First and Fast

First and Fast

Outpace Your Competitors, Lead Your Markets, and Accelerate Growth

Stuart Cross

BUSINESS EXPERT PRESS

First and Fast: Outpace Your Competitors, Lead Your Markets, and Accelerate Growth

Copyright © Business Expert Press, LLC, 2016

First published in 2016 by
Business Expert Press, LLC
222 East 46th Street, New York, NY 10017
www.businessexpertpress.com

ISBN-13: 978-1-63157-471-9 (paperback)
ISBN-13: 978-1-63157-472-6 (e-book)

Business Expert Press Strategic Management Collection

Collection ISSN: 1946-5637 (print)
Collection ISSN: 1946-5645 (electronic)

Cover and interior design by S4Carlisle Publishing Services Private Ltd., Chennai, India

First edition: 2016

10 9 8 7 6 5 4 3 2 1

Printed in the United States of America.

Dedication

To my wife, Scythia, and our three sons, Dylan, Archie, and Louis—thank you for making life so much more fun and rewarding than I ever thought possible.

—Stuart Cross

Abstract

For the past 30 years, business leaders have been exhorted to move faster and adopt a "ready, fire, aim" approach to the growth of their business. As the level of change and turbulence increases in all markets, all organizations must adapt—quickly!—or risk decline and decay. But what are the real behaviors, processes, and techniques that are critical to lead your organization at pace without creating confusion, frustration, and unnecessary risk?

First and Fast provides business leaders with a comprehensive and pragmatic set of tools and ideas to enable them to increase pace, build momentum, and accelerate growth in a systematic way. This book is written for business owners, chief executives, other senior executives and managers, consultants, and business advisors.

Readers will benefit by learning techniques to build and lead faster, more responsive organizations that are better able to grow and thrive in a fast-changing world. Among other things, they will know how to ensure that managers don't fall into the trap of sitting on yesterday's success when they should be shifting gears to deliver tomorrow's solutions, to demonstrate the necessary fast-paced leadership behaviors on a daily basis, and to transform their business from a "busy" organization to one that is genuinely the fastest and most effective in its market.

Keywords

#1 Goal, Business leader, Customer focus, Chief executive, Customer responsiveness, Fast-Lane innovation, Fast-paced implementation, Growth, Growth acceleration, Market leadership, Organizational pace, Organizational agility, Profit, Nothing fails like success, Rapid-fire strategy, 6-day strategy, Rapid results

Contents

Acknowledgments

I would like to thank all of my clients for providing both the inspiration and the fuel for this book.

I would also like to acknowledge all of the people who helped me in creating and completing the book, with particular thanks to Eric Dobby, a wonderful publisher who sadly passed away before the book was finished, Richard Baker and Andrew Stephenson, for their generosity of time and ideas, Alan Weiss, who gave me the confidence to start writing in the first place, and my wife, Scythia Cross, for playing the critical role of my English language teacher.

CHAPTER 1

Are You Fast or Irrelevant?

The Decline and Fall of Nokia

By February 2011, Stephen Elop had been the CEO of Nokia for nearly five months. The first non-Finnish director of the mobile communications giant, the former Adobe and Microsoft executive, had, since his appointment, been reviewing the company's declining performance and talking with the company's customers, workers, suppliers, shareholders, and partners. The results of Elop's review terrified him.

Nokia's once unassailable position across various segments of the mobile phone market had been rapidly eroded by competition from Apple in the smart phone segment, by the explosion in the share of Android in the mid-range market, and by Chinese manufacturers at the low-price end of the market. Symbian, the company's proprietary software, was seen as uncompetitive in many of the world's leading markets, particularly North America, and product development was both slow and lacked genuine innovation.

All of these issues had impacted negatively on results. Revenues were down from over €50 billion in 2008 to €42 billion in 2010, margins were in free-fall and operating profit had more than halved from nearly €5 billion to a little over €2 billion in the same period. Little wonder, perhaps, that the Board had looked outside of the company for its new chief executive.

Sitting at his desk at Nokia's global headquarters in Espoo, just outside Helsinki, Elop's mood was as dark as the long, seemingly endless Finnish winter nights. As he sat down to compose a memo to everyone inside the mobile phone giant, he realized he had to shake up the company's entire way of thinking. Elop didn't pull any punches in his analysis of the company's predicament, comparing Nokia's situation with a man on a burning oil platform in the middle of the Atlantic Ocean. The man was faced with the choice of burning to certain death or jumping into the icy waters. He decides to jump and suggests that Nokia needs to do the same.

Elop's "burning platform" memo is over 1,000 words in length. After writing it, Elop shared it with the organization ahead of the presentation of his new strategy for the business. Here are some key extracts:

- *We too, are standing on a "burning platform," and we must decide how we are going to change our behavior. And, we have more than one explosion—we have multiple points of scorching heat that are fuelling a blazing fire around us.*
- *The first iPhone shipped in 2007, and we still don't have a product that is close to their experience. Android came on the scene just over 2 years ago, and this week they took our leadership position in smartphone volumes. Unbelievable.*
- *Let's not forget about the low-end price range. In 2008, MediaTek supplied complete reference designs for phone chipsets, which enabled manufacturers in the Shenzhen region of China to produce phones at an unbelievable pace.*
- *While competitors poured flames on our market share, what happened at Nokia? We fell behind, we missed big trends, and we lost time. We now find ourselves years behind.*
- *At the low-end price range, Chinese OEMs are cranking out a device much faster than, as one Nokia employee said only partially in jest, "the time that it takes us to polish a PowerPoint presentation."*
- *Our competitors aren't taking our market share with devices; they are taking our market share with an entire ecosystem.*
- *I believe we have lacked accountability and leadership to align and direct the company through these disruptive times. We had a series of misses. We haven't been delivering innovation fast enough. We're not collaborating internally.*

You can feel Elop's frustration with the organization, can't you? He points to a lack of accountability and leadership, ineffective decision making, insipid innovation, and a lack of collaboration across Nokia over a period of time. But the memo points to one factor, above all others, that drove the company's decline: a lack of speed. In each market segment—the high-end, the mid-range, and the low-end—Elop identifies faster, more agile competitors getting ahead of Nokia and accelerating away.

The day following Elop's memo, he shared his refreshed strategy for the Nokia phones business. Alongside radical changes to the company's leadership, cost reductions, shifts in production and lay-offs, Elop's big strategic move consisted of a partnership with Microsoft that would lead to Nokia abandoning its in-house Symbian software and, instead, adopting the Windows Phone software in all its smart phones. Recognizing that Apple's iOS and Google's Android systems were now dominating the market, Nokia had little choice but to find a way of partnering with the #3 software provider, Microsoft.

Despite the initial hopes that the strategic partnership would help the two companies challenge Apple and Google, the results simply didn't follow. Even though Nokia's new Lumia phones received decent reviews, their level of innovation was still not enough to seriously disrupt the two market leaders. Nokia had simply fallen too far behind to have a chance of catching up. As shown in Figure 1.1, Nokia's smart phone market share had fallen from its high of over 50 percent in early 2007 to just 3 percent of global smart phone sales by mid-2013. Nokia's strategic partnership

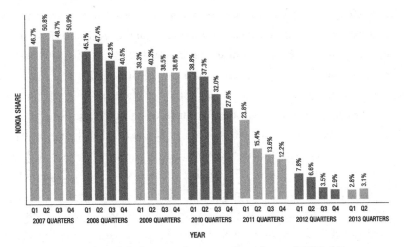

Figure 1.1 Nokia global smartphone market share, 2007–13

Source: Statista.

with Microsoft had had no noticeable impact on that decline. The company's financial performance followed the slide in share and in 2012 the company recorded an operating loss of over €2 billion.

The further decline of Nokia's phone business led to its sale to Microsoft for $7 billion in September 2013. In a little over five years, Nokia had gone from being the seemingly unassailable leader of the mobile phone market to a near irrelevance that the holding company's board of directors was more than happy to sell. The Nokia Company still carries on, but it now focuses on network infrastructure services, mapping and location services, and technology development. Mobile phones—and Stephen Elop—have left the Finnish giant for good.

What's Driving the Need for Speed?

Nokia operates in a fast-moving, highly dynamic market, driven by disruptive technological innovation. Schumpeter's "gales of creative destruction" are as common and as devastating in the mobile phone market as hurricanes and tropical storms are in the Caribbean and surrounding areas at the end of each summer season. In both cases, you know that storms will happen and major damage will result, but it's far harder to predict when and where they will take place with any certainty.

But what about other markets? Are companies in less turbulent sectors able to keep up with, anticipate, and respond to changes in their markets any more effectively? If you look at the list of the biggest corporations in the United States, as set out in the Standard & Poor's Top 100 index, you will find some of the bluest of blue chip businesses that America has to offer, and which operate in a wide variety of markets.

It seems almost inconceivable that such strong and vibrant companies could ever be fundamentally threatened or face issues that their executive teams can't manage. The 2014 list includes corporate behemoths such as American Express, Boeing, Caterpillar, Procter & Gamble, Coca-Cola, Disney, McDonald's, Wal-Mart, and IBM. Indeed, eight years earlier in 2006, the list looked equally impressive. Unfortunately, however, 38 of the Top 100 U.S. corporations from 2006 have fallen out of the Top 100.

While some of these corporations have slipped just outside the Top 100, the decline of others, such as Radio Shack, has been so severe that they have lost their independence. In fact, for 18 of these 37 businesses, their removal from the S&P 100 is because they are no longer independent publicly quoted corporations. Some, including Merrill Lynch, Anheuser Busch, Black & Decker, and National Semiconductor, were acquired by rivals; others, including Heinz, Harrah's, and Clear Channel Communications, were acquired by private equity institutions; and two from this list of corporate giants—Eastman Kodak and Lehman Brothers—had to file for bankruptcy.

In other words, in the space of just eight years, nearly 40 percent of the biggest companies in the United States were no longer members of the S&P 100, and nearly 20 percent of these businesses had lost their independence. The flip side of this decline is the rise of other corporations that came on to the list. Interestingly, the world's largest corporation, Apple, was not a member of the Top 100 in 2006 and neither were Amazon, eBay, Capital One, CVS, Nike, or Visa.

The lesson is that nothing lasts forever. If some of the biggest, strongest, and most powerful corporations can decline so rapidly, then no company is safe. For those businesses that are able to act with speed and agility, there are huge opportunities for growth, but for those that remain rooted in old ways of working and organizing, the future is bleak and you run the risk of becoming irrelevant. The whole purpose of this book is to ensure that your company is in the former group and not the latter.

The acceleration in the rate of environmental change and risk facing every business is summarized by five key trends:

1. Technological Acceleration

Economic and commercial growth has always been driven by technological innovation. The Industrial Revolution in England, for instance, was led and underpinned by advances including the flying shuttle, the spinning jenny, a national network of canals, trains and a national rail network, and, most critically, the steam engine. Each of these, and countless other inventions, catapulted Britain to the biggest economy in the world. Between 1700 and 1900, the U.K. population exploded from a little over 6 million to 42 million, a sevenfold increase, and the economy saw more than a 10-fold increase over the same period.

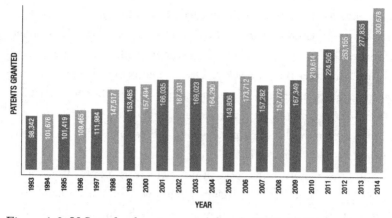

Figure 1.2 U.S. technology patents granted, 1993–2012

Source: U.S. Patents and Trademarks Office.

Technology's capacity to transform industries, markets, and even entire economies and societies is even more relevant today as it was in the 19th century. Figure 1.2 shows the number of utility (technological) patents that were granted by the U.S. Patent and Trademark Office between 1993 and 2012. Over that period, the number of patents granted grew from 98,000 to more than 250,000. Led by R&D arms of major multinational corporations including IBM, Samsung, Canon, Sony and Panasonic, this acceleration in the sheer scale of technology development shows no sign of slowing down.

Faster processing, growing memory storage and computing power, lower costs, greater interpersonal and interorganizational connectivity through mobile and cloud-based applications is reshaping both business and society in general. The remaining four drivers are themselves driven, in large part, by the continuing revolution in digital technology, and, as mentioned below, they demand businesses—and business leaders—that are increasingly agile, adaptive, and fast.

2. Leftfield Competition

If you look at a list of the world's top retailers, the top 5 has remained relatively constant over the past decade. In 2015, for instance, *The Global Powers of Retailing*, an annual report from accountancy firm, Deloitte, lists the Top 5 as Wal-Mart (United States), CostCo (United States), Carrefour (France), Schwarz (Germany) and Tesco (United Kingdom), with Metro (Germany) and Kroger (United States), filling the next two slots. This analysis may lead you to think that the retail industry is relatively stable: but you would be wrong, very wrong. Just outside the Top 10, with 2013 revenues of $74 billion and a five-year growth rate of over 26 percent per annum is a retailer without a single store. Since its launch in 1995, Amazon has reshaped the global retail landscape, directly impacting on customer service, home delivery, pricing, and ranging decisions of virtually every other retailer.

From its initial role as a new-start irritant to the major players, it is now one of the fastest-growing players in the world's Top 100 list and the thought leader for the industry. If you're a retail executive looking to improve your customer proposition, it is almost inconceivable that you can do this without first referring to Amazon's offer. Starting with the company's attack on traditional bookstores and music retailers, Amazon's convenience, range authority, and low prices have helped to extend the company's participation into virtually all retail categories. Although it has not previously competed directly in grocery, the biggest retail sector, this is likely to change with the roll out of AmazonFresh, delivering fresh products to its customers alongside its other, higher-value and higher-margin product categories.

Retail is not alone in facing new, leftfield competition. New forms of competition and the entrance of new, nontraditional players are now driving innovation in most markets. These upstart competitors come from one of five core categories:

1. **Channel Revolutionaries.** Amazon's success has been based on its focus on the online channel. Exploiting alternative channels has driven disruption in other markets, too. First Direct, a U.K. bank, for example, was first established in the 1980s as a telephone-only banking business, and rapidly set the standard for customer service and convenience.

2. **Cross-border Raiders.** The quality and quantity of international competition continues to grow, however, at an exponential rate. Trade agreements, technology developments, and the rapid growth

of many economies have ensured that new market entrants can set up and do business on a global scale more easily than ever before. As we have seen, for example, a key element of Nokia's struggle was its inability to deal with newer, faster, and cheaper Chinese competition.

3. **Business Model Innovators.** The dominance of mass European and U.S. airlines, such as BA, American and Delta, has been overthrown in the past decade by the rise of airlines with two types of business model. First, low-fare airlines have undercut these traditional players, attracted new customers to the market, and attracted more value-focused business flyers. Second, Asian airlines including Singapore, Emirates, and Etihad have redefined luxury air travel by providing an amazing experience for affluent passengers. The traditional airlines have struggled to keep pace with this twin attack of innovation, and have lost customers, market share, and profits.

4. **Market Redefiners.** Part of the genius of the Starbucks proposition was its redefinition of a café or coffee shop from being a commodity service to a lifestyle choice for everyone. How else can you explain the fact that 250-pound truck drivers seem happy to pay $5 for a coffee, even if it is a skinny latte? Howard Schulz, the CEO of Starbucks, didn't accept the coffee shop market as it was; he redefined it into something new.

5. **Digital Intermediaries.** Digital technology has enabled a revolution across different agency businesses, including travel agents, estate agents, and financial advisors. In the travel business, for example, families wanting to go on vacation no longer talk to their local travel agent and ask them to help organize the trip. Instead, they will open their iPads and click on their TripAdvisor app to find the best deals and the best-rated resorts. From its head office in Needham MA, and founded in 2000, TripAdvisor has rapidly become the world's leading travel website, with annual revenues of $1.3 billion and attracting over 280 million visits each month. As a result, the traditional travel agency business has all but disappeared.

3. *Shortening Investment and Product Life Cycles*

When I first became Head of Strategy for Boots the Chemists in 2000, the company looked for a payback on investment in its new stores within seven years. As a result, we diligently prepared financial forecasts and risk assessments for each new store, hoping that it would pass the seven-year hurdle. Our risk assessments didn't include any kind of impact assessment of the scale of the 2008 crash, the explosion in online sales or the rise of Amazon. In short, they failed to take account of some of the key retail drivers of the past decade: our assessments were painstakingly done but were, essentially, useless.

I'm not sure what payback period Boots currently looks for but I'm sure that it will be a lot less than seven years. Many of my retail clients now look for payback on their investment in new stores of less than two or three years, and one has an 18-month hurdle. In a little over 10 years, I estimate that the investment cycle in new retail stores in the United Kingdom has more than halved. New stores need to succeed quickly and, at the same time, retailers are looking to reduce the up-front investment required to deliver that success.

It's similar with new product development. According to one academic study, for example, the three generations of phones—traditional landline phones, cell phones, and smart phones—demonstrate acceleration in consumer adoption rates.[1] Taking 40 percent penetration as a reasonable indicator of market maturity, it took landline telephones 64 years to achieve 40 percent penetration of U.S. households, while it took mobile phones a little over 17 years to achieve the same level of adoption, and smart phones just 10 years. If you are an executive in the phone business, you had decades to sort yourself out to win in the landline phone market but just a matter of months to find a winning edge in the smart phone market. That's why Nokia's decline was so dramatic. The company was simply too slow out of the smart phone blocks and that initial hesitation cost the company its independence.

4.   The End of the "Developing" World

Hans Rosling is a Professor of Global Health at the Karolinska Instiutet in Sweden. He is focused on global health trends and the economic, technological, social and demographic forces that drive them, and on using the

---

[1]*"Are smart phones spreading faster than any technology in human history?"* Michael DeGusta, MIT Technology Review, May 2012.

insights he gains to dispel common myths about the so-called developing world. Professor Rosling points out that, unlike 50 years ago, you cannot now split the nations of the world into "developed" and "developing" countries. The situation is far more subtle and nuanced, and countries span a spectrum of wealth and prosperity with most of the world's population living in countries that lie somewhere in the middle of this continuum, in countries such as China, Brazil, India, Mexico, Turkey, and Thailand.

Consequently, half the world's economic output, and most of the economic growth, is now generated outside of North America and Western Europe, and these countries are reaching economic maturity almost twice as fast as the old economies did. The share of global GDP that was generated by fast-growing markets (China, India, Russia, Brazil, Mexico, South Korea, Turkey, and Indonesia) economies grew from just 9 percent to 25 percent between 2000 and 2011. At the same time, the "developed" markets' share fell from 78 percent of global GDP to 63 percent. Goldman Sachs forecast that the fast-growing markets' share of global GDP will climb to 46 percent by 2050, while the "developed" markets' share could shrink to just 31 percent.

The rapid shift in economic power creates both challenges and opportunities for companies in almost equal measure. The higher levels of economic growth across will create new markets for business, but only if you are agile and focused enough to exploit them. As we have seen with Nokia, one of the key problems for that business was its low share of business in new, emerging Chinese and Asian markets, reducing its overall market strength.

Nokia's challenges were exacerbated by the second challenge that emerges from the rise of these economies: the creation of new competitors. For Nokia, companies such as Media Tek and Huawei Technologies, developed offerings that were not only attractive to customers in these emerging and fast-growing markets, but which also threatened Nokia's core markets too. The pace at which they were able to innovate and bring new offerings to market was a crucial factor driving their success, and as the level of competition increases, pace will continue to grow as a source of competitive advantage.

5. Customer Power and Brand Fragility

Who owns your brand? The answer is important because it reflects your beliefs about how brands work. Brands certainly have a value and, according to Interbrand, the world's five most valuable brands—Apple, Google, Coca-Cola, IBM, and Microsoft—had a combined brand value of over $400 billion in 2013. But if you think about a brand in the same way as you think about other assets such as land, property, patents or equipment, then you also think that you, the brand owner, are in control.

Brands really only exist in the minds and beliefs of your target customers, and yet they can be your most valuable asset. Only when your customers' perceptions of your brand are associated with positive views about the quality, reliability, performance, enjoyment, integrity, value, image and emotional impact of your products, services, and organization, you are likely to have a valuable brand.

One company that is not in Interbrand's Top 5, or even its Top 100, is BP. The company fell out of favor, and saw its brand value collapse, following the Deepwater Horizon disaster. It was not so much the horrific explosion, the needless deaths of 11 crewmen on the rig and the largest offshore oil spill in U.S. history that was the cause of BP's brand nightmare, but the slow, ineffectual reaction from the company's leadership team to the unfolding events. While the CEO, Tony Hayward, was complaining that "You know, I'd like my life back," people across the world could see for themselves a continuous TV and webcast video of the oil coming out of the broken pipes. And as the oil plume became bigger, and BP's list of excuses longer, the level of trust in the brand melted away.

BP is, perhaps, an extreme example, but it highlights that the balance of power between sellers and buyers has shifted significantly to the buyers. Media coverage exacerbated and accelerated the decline of the BP brand, and our 24/7 access to TV news and social media has step-changed the level of knowledge at customers' fingertips. It only takes a click or two for your customers to understand what other customers really think about you—either fairly or unfairly. They can also easily access information about how your company is run, the background and integrity of your key officers, and the alignment between your brand values and your corporate actions.

As a result, consumers can force executives to make decisions to protect their brand far more easily and rapidly than ever before. In 2013, for example, Starbucks "voluntarily" paid £10 million in corporate taxes in response to a largely online outcry over its low reported U.K. profits, driven, it appears, by perfectly legal accounting policies that enable the company to focus its profitability in lower-tax countries. Similarly, in 2011 it took a little over a month for Armani and Versace to remove sand-blasted denim from their ranges, following an online petition of 38,000 people protesting against the process, while, in the same year, 75,000 negative tweets to Reed Hastings, the CEO of Netflix, was all it took to force him to e-mail a personal apology to millions of Netflix subscribers and reverse his decision to split the brand's streaming (Netflix) and DVD (Qwickster) services.

Why are Companies Still Too Slow?

These external drivers of pace and change might suggest that there is little that companies can do to prevent their own decline; they are simply pieces of flotsam and jetsam being thrown around on capricious market tides. Yet some companies continue to survive and thrive. Corporate giants such as P&G, GE, and Walgreens may have their ups and downs, but they continue to attract and retain customers, find ways to grow, and generate strong returns.

If they can do it, why can't everyone? The problems of adapting to the pace of change are, it seems, internal rather than external. In short, many companies are still too slow because of a seeming inability of leaders and their organizations to sustainably act at a pace that is equal to or faster than the pace of change that surrounds them. There are five underlying reasons for this situation, as described below.

1.   Organizing for Last Century's Realities

A key problem for many businesses is how they are organized. Most corporate organizations continue to be based, on the whole, on a 20th-century model of control and hierarchy. If you compare the way businesses are organized and run today, compared with 10, 20 or even 30 years ago, the only real difference, in many companies, is that managers have to travel more, run bigger teams, work longer hours, and somehow find a way to deal with the explosion of e-mail and mobile communication.

This means, for instance, that your organization probably has several layers of management between the executive team and front line colleagues, takes an annual planning approach to its strategy, operations and financials, requires more junior staff members to seek sign-off and approval for most significant decisions from those in more senior positions and has teams of people, in Stephen Elop's words, "polishing PowerPoint presentations" for the senior team rather than getting on with delivering new growth and value for customers.

As with carbon monoxide, which kills by replacing the oxygen in a room with a poison that has no smell or taste, unnecessary organizational controls are a pace-killer that are mostly unseen and difficult to detect. At a major U.K. services business, for example, the managing director of one of the smaller divisions, with supposedly full profit and loss accountability, decided to develop a new marketing campaign to attract and retain customers. It took him over 12 months to get the campaign off the ground, as he needed the group marketing director's approval to release the funds required, and the marketing team simply had different priorities. In reality, the divisional managing director did not have full profit and loss accountability—despite what the group chief executive believed—and the lack of clarity about this single decision right created a year-long delay in the delivery of his division's growth strategy. Multiply this situation across other decisions rights—IT systems, infrastructure, product development, talent acquisition—and it quickly becomes clear how a lack of clarity, and simplicity, over accountabilities can turn an organizational racehorse into a pit pony.

2. The Fear of Failure Paradox

A retail CEO once invited me to the opening of a new concept store. The company had made a big investment in the new concept and so there were high hopes that this trial would succeed. The store looked great, and the initial customer reaction was extremely positive. I turned to one of the project managers and asked him if he'd been closely involved with the development. "Well," he replied laconically, "It's too early to say." Behind his witticism was an understanding that his business demanded immediate success and had an unwillingness to accept any sort of failure, even when testing new concepts. Failure was not a learning opportunity; it was simply an opportunity to seek a new career. Unsurprisingly, this business did not have a strong track record of either innovation or pace. Managers did not want to stick their head above the parapet and take a risk on a new product or initiative, as the chances were they would be shot at.

But there is a paradox here. The desire to avoid risk and potential failure can create the very conditions that make failure more likely. There is no growth without risk, and yet many successful companies seem to forget the behaviors and attitudes that created their success. In the 1980s, for example, Lotus, despite its success from its Lotus 1-2-3 spreadsheet software and its subsequent employment of many highly qualified managers, was struggling to develop a new breakthrough product.

The chairman, who had become increasingly frustrated with the executive team, ran a test. He took the resumes of the company's first employees, many of whom had track records of major risk-taking, changed the names, and sent them through to the HR department. Not one was asked to the company for interview. Instead, it took a stand-alone team, located away from the corporate head office, to develop the company's next success, Lotus Notes.[2]

3. Incrementalism

If you're unwilling to risk failure and want to ensure that you always reach your target, then you will only ever set goals you know you will achieve. Consequently, you are almost inevitably focused on incremental, rather than step-change goals. And, if you only ever want to improve sales, customer satisfaction and loyalty, operational productivity or profit by a few percentage points, then you can usually make that happen by doing what you do already.

---

[2]See "*Weird Ideas That Work: 11 ½ practices for promoting, managing and sustaining innovation*" by Robert Sutton, The Free Press, 2002.

What's more, incremental targets tend to be more inward looking. As we've already seen, however, in chaotic, rapidly changing markets, if you simply stick to what you're already doing, no matter how successful that might be currently, you will, at some point, be overtaken by events and by competitors who are faster, more agile, and more focused on creating the future.

The result of a focus on incremental improvement is an organization that is planning-led. Management's need for control overrides any desire for innovation, stifling action, and personal initiative. At one of my clients, the annual planning process once started nine months before the start of the year concerned, or 21 months before the end of the year in question. Managers and staff were asked by a central planning team to put forward their ideas for growth nearly two years before they might be implemented! It was little wonder that the company's actual rate of growth was anemic; its ability to respond to new emerging opportunities and developments in its market was virtually nil.

All of the high-paced companies that I've encountered have something in common: a focus on action. Rather than being constrained by central, top-down planning, managers are encouraged to take action and make things happen. As we shall see, this doesn't mean that there isn't any control. But it is fair to say that a certain level of chaos is required to survive, let alone thrive, in any 21st-century business. Plans have their place, but action and effective performance management are far more important.

4. "Yes"

Perhaps the most dangerous word that can pass a senior executive's lips is "Yes." It is also, of course, the most powerful and valuable word, but the irony is that if you keep saying "Yes" to all the good ideas you and your people have, you're really saying "No" to rapid results, or at least saying "Not for a while." I remember talking to the CEO of a major British retailer and asking him about the company's strategic agenda. He told me that he had agreed 27 priorities with his executive team. So, I asked him what these priorities were and, after sharing his top seven or eight, he became stuck and couldn't remember the final 20! If you can't name your priorities it's unlikely that you're going to be able to deliver them, and the company reviewed and reassessed its major projects soon after.

It's just not possible for any organization to maintain focus if you are constantly asking your teams and your managers to take on another good idea when they still haven't delivered last week's priority. Back in 2004, for example, U.K. retail giant, M&S, was struggling to compete against key rivals such as Next, as well as a much stronger, value offer from the major grocers, led by Asda-Walmart. The Board hired a new CEO, Stuart Rose, and one of his first actions was to cull the 31 "strategic projects" the company was pursuing. As Sir Stuart wrote soon after, "The company was lurching from one strategy to another. If a strategy didn't work by Friday, a new one was initiated on Monday. The staff became demoralized by the onslaught of ever-shifting, unclear messages and strategies, which led to more bad decisions about product and further damaged the way M&S dealt with customers. It was a rapid downward spiral."[3] In other words, the previous CEO's inability to say "No" to a new initiative, and his desire to say "Yes," led directly to a lack of progress at the company and, even worse, contributed to its decline.

5. *Sticking with Your Historic Golden Eggs*

Perhaps ironically, the companies that are in the biggest danger of becoming irrelevant are those that are already relatively successful. New businesses, and those in a crisis, know that they must act differently, move more quickly, and exploit new opportunities better than their competitors. Companies that are already successful often have a different mindset. They are far more likely to be focused on how they can maintain their position in the market, protect cash flows, and maximize the returns they enjoy from their current market advantage for as long as possible. Their problem is that companies that are able to align their capabilities and build advantages to perfectly meet current market opportunities cannot necessarily adapt to meet tomorrow's. In other words, nothing fails like success.

---

[3]*"Back in fashion: How we're reviving a British icon,"* Stuart Rose, Harvard Business Review, May 2007.

A management approach of protecting current performance and avoiding the aggressive pursuit of new, and potentially threatening, opportunities may seem like the low risk option, but in reality it can often end up being a higher risk choice. Kodak, Olivetti and, now, Nokia have all ended up in a worse market and financial position as a result of their unwillingness and inability to change, adapt, and innovate at a pace that is equal to or greater than the pace of change in your market.

Shifting Focus from Perfection to Pace

Nokia's leadership team found out too late that the dynamic nature of modern markets mean that you can no longer build a fortress to defend and expect to survive intact; you must, instead, leave your citadel and carry on attacking. You must, as an organization, feel the wind in your hair from your own acceleration, rather than the breeze created by your rivals as they speed by. The organization had become infected with a condition that I call "perfection addiction," which inhibits managers and leaders from making the decisions and taking the actions that would move their businesses forward. *Perfection addiction* is an insidious condition that impacts all areas of an organization and appears to have helped to create the arrogance, inertia, and fear that prevented Nokia from building on its previous success. The company couldn't move because it needed committees from across the company to cross the t's and dot the i's on every decision, even when it was clear that the leaders of the different functions had very different ideas about the best way forward.

Nokia's fall from grace was not inevitable, however. The flip side of the company's decline was the dramatic success of many of its rivals, including Samsung, Apple, Google/Android, MediaTek, and Huwaei Technologies. Unlike Nokia, each of these companies were able to anticipate and adapt to rapidly changing market conditions, build and embed a high-speed innovation pipeline, and accelerate revenues and returns. The five brakes to growth, mentioned above, simply didn't apply to these businesses. But I don't think that it's sufficient to simply exhort you to build a 21st-century organization, remove your fear of failure, avoid planning perfectionism, learn to say "No" more often, and recognize and act on the perils of success.

The $100 trillion question is *how* do you build those skills, attitudes, and behaviors across your leadership team and across your organization? What are the specific details of what's required, how do you make them happen, and how do you make them stick? That is what this book is focused on. My aim is to give you pragmatic tools and approaches that will enable you to step-change the level of speed in your business. Not only do I want your organization to be first, I want it to be fast.

Figure 1.3 identifies the six key factors that turn slow, lethargic organizations into agile, responsive, and, above all, fast businesses. I call these "The Six Speed Drivers." Working on any one of them has the potential to step-change your company's pace, but improving all six drivers can transform your potential and your future. In the coming chapters, we will review each of the drivers and focus on how you can best develop the

Figure 1.3 The six speed drivers

pace to lead your markets and accelerate away from your competitors. We will set out practical approaches that you can use to increase your rate and impact of innovation, develop more productive relationships with your customers, organize for speed and agility, implement major initiatives at pace, and ensure that your strategy remains relevant and capable of driving rapid growth. But we will start at the beginning, and understand the cultural and leadership foundations that are necessary to become an organization that is both first and fast.

CHAPTER 2

Creating a High-Speed, High-Growth Culture

Avoiding the Cultural Danger Zone

In Chapter 1, we described the decline and fall of Nokia's mobile phone business. When Stephen Elop realized that Nokia had to radically change in order to survive, he asked the Nokia organization in his "burning platform" e-mail, "How did we get to this point? Why did we fall behind when the world around us evolved? This is what I have been trying to understand. I believe at least some of it has been due to our attitude inside Nokia. We poured gasoline on our own burning platform." In other words, Elop believed that, over time, the values and beliefs that permeated the Nokia organization inhibited the level of decisiveness and innovation that had created its previous success.

Figure 2.1 shows a typical corporate life cycle, and the three potential phases. In the early, high-growth stages, the company is focused on refining, replicating, and extending its success. Managers are typically focused on growth acceleration and the whole organization is engaged in moving at speed. When you talk to managers and executives who have been through this stage, they often talk about the exhilaration of the experience. It feels like you are taking on the world—and winning! It's little wonder that serial entrepreneurs get bored with their success and want to repeat the feelings of excitement that young, high-growth businesses can deliver. Companies undergoing early stage success have a culture of innovation, courage, and hope that enhances the speed and pace of the organization.

Companies in decline can also have a high-speed, action-focused culture. The need to reinvent the business before the decline becomes

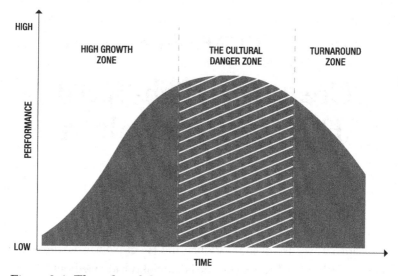

Figure 2.1 The cultural danger zone

terminal leads management to leave no stone unturned. Indeed, some managers are turnaround specialists, who move from one struggling organization to another, looking to make the necessary cuts and decisions that previous management teams haven't been willing to take. Companies in decline aren't nearly as much fun as the start-ups—there is no time for table football competitions or skateboarding around the offices—but with active management they do move at pace.

In many ways, the real danger zone for businesses is in the mature growth phase, where the early sprint of growth has been replaced by the slog of incremental gains. As the pace of growth slows down, management can make one of three choices:

1. Ignore the decline in growth rate, and continue to believe, instead, that what has driven your historic success will keep you successful in the future. This choice often results from collective arrogance. The U.S. car giants, for instance, spent many years during the 1970s and 1980s in denial about the threat and growth of their Japanese rivals, incorrectly believing that patriotic U.S. customers would always, in the end, buy American.

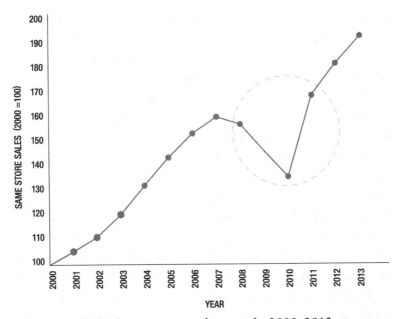

Figure 2.2 Starbucks same store sales growth, 2000–2012

Source: Company Annual Reports.

2. Accept the decline in growth rate, and shift the focus of the business onto margin management and defensive revenue protection initiatives. This is the stage when executives talk about the business going "ex-growth" and start to highlight improvements in the ratios of return on capital and return on sales rather than actual profit and growth improvements.

3. Decide to act before the slowdown in growth turns into a full-scale decline. In this situation, managers act ahead of the curve and take proactive steps to reinvigorate the business, find new growth opportunities, and drive their company's next phase of success.

One company that took the third option was Starbucks. Figure 2.2 shows the revenues of the business between 1995 and 2014. Led by Howard Schultz as CEO between 1998 and 2000, Schultz then decided to become the nonexecutive chairman of the business, only to return eight years later as the company's performance started to falter. As shown in the chart, the actual decline in sales took place after Schultz's return, but the warning signs had been there throughout 2007. Like-for-like sales growth—that is the sales growth of stores opened more than 12 months—was in decline, falling from 10 percent in 2004 to 5 percent in 2007 (these same store sales were to fall by 3 percent in 2008), and, even more importantly, the share price had halved as investors began to realize that the company's ability to grow year on year was under threat.

As Schultz came back into the hot seat in January 2008, he, like Stephen Elop was to do later at Nokia, wrote a memo to all of the company's staff. In that letter, Schultz noted, "If we take an honest look at Starbucks today, then we know that we are emerging from a period in which we invested in infrastructure ahead of the growth curve. Although necessary, it led to bureaucracy. We will now shift our emphasis back onto customer-facing initiatives, better aligning our back-end costs with our business model."[1] In other words, Schultz realized that organizational power had shifted from the partners in the stores to the professional head office managers. This is a common trend among successful, high-growth companies, but professional managers tend to be more risk averse and far less entrepreneurial than the managers and leaders that built the company in the first place.

It is the stealth-like corporate takeover by these professional managers that can shift the culture and values of businesses away from pace, innovation and growth to risk management, analysis and protection. Most companies lie neither in the high-growth phase or the decline phase; they lie in the low growth, plateau phase, otherwise known as the cultural danger zone. If your business lies in this zone, it is essential that you proactively manage the culture of your organization so that you avoid turning a slow-down in growth into complete failure. The best way to do that is to adopt the best elements of the start-up company cultures and to systematically tackle the most likely cultural roadblocks to your success. We'll deal with each of these in turn in the next two sections.

---

[1] As reported by Bloomberg Business, http://www.bloomberg.com/bw/stories/2008-01-07/howard-schultzs-memobusinessweek-business-news-stock-market-and-financial-advice, accessed October 2015.

Act Like a Start-up and Adopt a Challenger Mind-set

Launched in the late 1990s by three Cambridge University graduates, Innocent Drinks has become a $300-million business producing smoothies, juices, and vegetable meals for sale through supermarkets and other major retailers. By 2012, Innocent was selling over 2 million smoothies per week, had become Europe's leading smoothie brand, had gained over 60 percent U.K. market share, and was delivering annual profits of over $25 million. Unsurprisingly, the business had attracted the attention of competitors and brand owners and in 2012 Coca-Cola acquired a 90 percent share of the business, which it valued at over $500 million.

Innocent Drinks delivered rapid, profitable growth and value creation in a little over a decade. The company didn't achieve its high-speed success playing by the rules of the leading incumbents in the drinks market. Coca-Cola and Pepsi have created huge brand recognition and loyalty in the soft drinks market through massive and sustained investment in above-the-line advertising. This investment and loyalty enables them to adopt a strong negotiating position with retailers who, as a result, allow Coca-Cola's and Pepsi's brands to dominate the displays in the soft drinks area of their stores.

The three partners behind Innocent Drinks had only a tiny fraction of the resources they would need to play Coca-Cola or Pepsi at that game. What's more, they realized that, given the huge number of smaller brands in this market, Innocent would have to do something different to set itself apart from the myriad of other niche players, let alone the market giants. At the heart of Innocent's distinctiveness and success was a different set of values and a brand personality that skillfully combined ethical and commercial elements into a compelling proposition. Underneath the brand statement of "Tastes Good. Does Good," Innocent's stated values are natural, entrepreneurial, responsible, commercial, and generous.

In other words, fast-paced businesses like Innocent Drinks look, act, and feel different from their more leisurely rivals: their organizational structures are different, their processes are different, their people are different, and their level of activity is different. But underpinning all these differences is a distinct set of values and beliefs. It is these cultural differences that create and sustain the other variances, and without them your company's speed of growth and improvement will atrophy.

There are four key attitudes that underpin companies with a "challenger mind-set" and which drives their energy, pace, and relentlessness.

1. **Acting Fearlessly.** As the leader of every "challenger" business knows, there is no growth without risk. In fact, a *Business Week* survey of leading Silicon Valley entrepreneurs found that the #1 top tactic they believed drove their success was their ability to "experiment fearlessly." So, when I come across managers in a company who avoid, rather than manage risk, it's a major signal to me that their organization is likely to lack the speed to succeed in their chosen markets. In fact, many successful companies seem to forget the behaviors and attitudes that created their success and, as a result, fail to try anything that has a chance of failure. If you cannot accept failure, you are unlikely to see too much innovation, no matter how much money you throw at it. Innocent, like most "challenger" businesses had its fair share of failures and relied on the ongoing commitment of its leaders to drive its ultimate success. For example, in 2007 the company started to supply its drinks to McDonalds, but after a series of trials, McDonalds pulled the plug on the idea as its customers failed to buy in sufficient quantities. One truth of breakthrough ideas is that they will be noticed, and will receive criticism, particularly if there is less than 100 percent chance of success. Many managers, through experience, fear criticism and only pursue ideas where there is already mass customer support. As a business leader, overcoming these fears starts with you. As Jonathan Warburton, the Managing Director of the family-owned Warburton's bakery noted, "One of the great responsibilities of owner-drivers is to stick their necks out and be seen to take risks, because they're fireproof. What chance is there of the hired help taking risks if the guys at the top won't stick their necks out?" *In what ways do you encourage your managers to take prudent risks and act fearlessly?*

2. **Becoming the Ideas Leader for Your Market.** Challengers don't often have the luxury of huge marketing budgets, so look for new avenues to tell their story. One way to overcome the marketing challenge is to become the ideas leader of your market. Ideas are newsworthy, and are commented on in the media, providing free advertising for your business and your brand. Innocent, for example, challenged

the concept of modern business, talking about their role as a force for good in the world, as much as the benefits of their products and services. For example, in addition to the Innocent Foundation, which is funded by 10 percent of the annual profits of the business, Innocent launched "The Big Knit," which involves volunteers knitting tiny woolen hats for their smoothie bottles at Christmas with the business donating 10 pence to the charity Age UK for every one of these bottles that are sold. This campaign allows Innocent to talk about the importance of keeping the elderly warm during the winter months, as well as enabling people to get involved in the scheme, in a way that attracts positive media attention. Your ideas don't have to be charitable, however. Ryanair has historically had a far more edgy, colder personality, but has still achieved free publicity, for example, by raising the idea of removing toilets from their planes to free up space for more passengers on each flight. Similarly, Amazon was the first retailer to raise the idea of using drones to deliver products, leading to many free column inches of newspaper discussion in line with their strategic aim of improving the convenience and speed of product delivery. *What are you doing to become the leader of new, innovative ideas for your markets?*

3. **Erring on the Side of Cannibalization.** Economist Joseph Schumpeter called the symbiotic link between innovation and the elimination of existing forms of value "creative destruction." If you aren't willing to destroy, you aren't willing to innovate or, in turn, act like a challenger. All technology companies know that they must consistently add new features at lower prices if they want to stay ahead in the market. While the same principles are true in other markets, some companies live in fear of cannibalization while others set out to make their own products obsolete before the competition does it for them. Gillette, for example, has consistently strengthened its leadership in razors through its willingness to make its existing ranges redundant by creating a stream of innovations. The Sensor razor created the initial breakthrough, before being superseded by the Mach3, which has, in turn, been overthrown by Fusion. Gillette already has clear plans for its next iteration when it launches a new range and this proactive approach helps drive the speed and momentum of the organization. Conversely, companies such as Kodak and Nokia that preferred to

focus on protecting their existing advantages and defending their existing technologies and products for as long as possible, lose speed and momentum over time and ultimately find that they no longer have the ability to accelerate their NPD pipeline once it becomes inevitable that their existing ranges are becoming obsolete. *Where are you willing to challenge your own success and cannibalize your revenues so that you can continue to accelerate growth?*

4. **Not Just Being Better, But Being Different.** Innocent had something different to offer consumers when it was launched. There were other smoothie brands, but the industry was in its infancy and Innocent led the way in growing the market. In most established markets, it is very difficult to offer something that is a little better than what is already being offered. Buyers of deodorants, pain relief tablets, yogurts, and many other commonly bought items have already made up their mind about their preferred brands. Your product or service may be slightly better than what is already on offer in the market, but unless it is massively superior to the incumbents' offerings, as the Dyson vacuum cleaner was, you're unlikely to make much impact on the market. Successful challengers, such as Innocent, Ryanair, Amazon, and Dyson, offer something that is radically new and different, meeting new and unmet needs, and forcing potential customers to reappraise their existing buying habits. Unsurprisingly, perhaps, Innocent has had less success with its fruit juice ranges than its smoothie products. Consumers have already decided which juice brand they prefer, but were open to a new product where they hadn't already decided on their preference. *How well do you ensure that your new products and services are radically different to anything else in the market, so that your target customers need to think again about their preferred supplier?*

The Cultural Traffic Jam: The Seven Most Likely Roadblocks

In recent years, I have had problems with my shoulders. Bony spurs have appeared, which impinge on some muscles, creating pain and weakness in equal measure. As the specialist kindly put it, "Stuart, it's a sign of growing up!" Organizational beliefs, habits, and mind-sets can quickly ossify in a similar way to my shoulders. Consequently, it is not enough simply to try and adopt the best of new start-up company beliefs and habits if you really want to avoid the cultural danger zone and continue to accelerate growth. In any relatively mature organization, you must also tackle the points of inertia, cut away the bony spurs of resistance, and free up your joints so that you can painlessly move with ease and speed once again.

Creating a fast-paced, dynamic organization means that you must, in reality, develop an environment that actively encourages and supports rapid decision making and actions, and that discourages prevarication, delay, inaction, and procrastination. But what are the environmental forces that create roadblocks to your goals of pace and speed? Here are seven of the most common and most intrusive roadblocks that I have come across. Tackle these seven issues and you will have made major strides in helping your organization to start sprinting again.

1. **Unclear Goals and Expectations.** It is obvious, perhaps, that behavioral change will not happen if people do not understand what new behaviors are expected of them. Yet, many organizational leaders become frustrated at a lack of organizational pace even though they haven't themselves articulated to their teams what success looks like. The CEO of a manufacturing client of mine once told me that his leadership team just wouldn't get fully on board in delivering the company's new strategy, and complained that he felt like he had to carry the whole organization on his back. As we discussed further, it became clear that the strategy had been developed by just two or three of the leadership team, and that little, if any, time had been devoted to engaging the rest of the senior managers on the way forward and the new behaviors required. As a result, we spent time refining the strategy with far wider involvement of the executive board, helping all the top team, and, in turn, their teams to understand the goals and to be actively involved in establishing their own targets and plans to deliver them. As a result, the new leadership behaviors the CEO wanted began to be displayed by the wider leadership team. *How have you shared and explained your expectations to your team, and how well do they understand what success actually looks like?*

2. **Fear of Failure.** Some managers are perfectionists and want things to be totally right before taking action, but in other organizations it is the fear that you will be called out by your boss for failure that prevents you taking action. At one major U.K. company I worked with, for instance, the CEO would publicly lambast his directors and managers in executive meetings for their mistakes. He was a talented manager who knew his business inside out, but his behavior put a stranglehold on the company's energy and pace. His criticisms weren't short, one-sentence put-downs, but five or ten minutes of intense criticism and, unsurprisingly, the leadership team didn't like to make decisions without the CEO's backing. As a result, instead of moving their initiatives forward at pace, even the most senior managers would only take the next step once the CEO had approved it. Ironically, the CEO complained that no one would make a decision and that everything in the company happened so slowly, but the root cause of the jam was the environment of fear that his own behavior had created. *What behaviors are causing a fear of failure in your organization?*

3. **The Planning and Analysis Reflex.** Some organizations like to shoot first and ask questions later. Action-driven people who, all things being equal, are only satisfied when they are doing stuff lead them. Other organizations are quite different. The environment creates a desire for managers to analyze every decision in great detail, looking at things from various angles and making sure that managers fully understand all the risks and potential pitfalls before pressing the "go" button. The analysis can take place at various levels in the hierarchy and managers seem to like nothing better than dissect ideas and proposals in the hope of finding problems and reasons not to implement them. In my experience, these analytical default behaviors are most prevalent in organizations where scientists, accountants, and lawyers form a major part of the leadership team. *What level of analysis is required before taking action on new ideas in your organization, and, if present, what is driving the analytical reflex?*

4. **Following the Rewards.** People tend to act in their own best self-interest. This means that they will minimize the behaviors that limit their rewards—which may be in the form of status, satisfaction, or

development as well as financial—and focus on the behaviors that maximize these rewards. Many companies struggle to truly become more innovative and entrepreneurial because the formal and informal reward systems are still focused on delivering "safe" profits. If you know that you're going to be punished for failure, for instance, your people will have little, if any, incentive to move outside your comfort zone and try out these new behaviors. *What rewards are your people pursuing, and how well aligned are these rewards to the behaviors you're looking to develop?*

5. **"My Agenda" Trumps "Our Agenda."** My example of passive resistance was an example of an individual pursuing his own agenda at the expense of the organization's strategy, but this was done undercover. The resistance can be more open, where managers and executives more deliberately and explicitly decide to follow their own priorities. International businesses, for instance, often struggle to align the priorities of their local country teams with the company's corporate initiatives, which is why they often end up creating hugely complex matrix organizations. At one of my corporate clients, country managers had only implemented 50 percent of the company's recent product innovations because they did not believe they were relevant to their local markets. They may have been right or wrong, but the lack of delivery of the corporate agenda significantly impeded the business in achieving its growth acceleration ambitions. Such behavior is not limited to international corporations, of course. I once worked with a mid-sized U.K. training business where several of the local offices failed to pursue strategic new growth opportunities because their local teams simply didn't feel comfortable delivering the new type of training involved. These managers' resistance wasn't passive, but the organization's mantra of local autonomy meant that it went unchallenged for over two years, allowing several other competitors to take the lead in exploiting the opportunity. *What steps have you taken to ensure that managers' agendas are in line with your corporate priorities?*

6. **Low Review Cadence.** In cycling, cadence represents the pedaling rate of the rider. The greater the revolutions of the pedals, the higher the cadence. Cyclists look to increase their cadence in order to

improve results. Pace and cadence are inextricably linked in business as well as cycling. If you are reviewing results quarterly, you will only get infrequent improvements to performance. The businesses that move the quickest are those that have the fastest and most effective review and feedback systems. The discipline of reviewing progress on your most important initiatives weekly, rather than monthly, for instance, can have a transformative effect on the speed and quality of implementation. Managers feel accountable for taking action if they know they are going to be asked about what's happened in the previous seven days. They also feel more committed to delivery with a higher review cadence, but only if there is a genuine environment of collective support, rather than a feeling of a court appearance. *What is the frequency and style of the reviews of your organization's most important initiatives and activities?*

7. **Passive Resistance.** The Managing Director of a retail business once charged me with developing a new growth strategy for the business. The strategy was signed off by the business and required the development of new retail formats. Try as I might, and despite public statements of support, however, I struggled to gain the active support of the buying teams to create the ranges and displays for these new formats, which, unsurprisingly, failed to achieve the sales growth targets we had set. It was only over 12 months later, when the Trading EVP left the business, that he finally told me that he hadn't really believed the strategy was the best way forward and had made sure the resources weren't made available. His resistance hadn't been out in the open, but had been undercover and to me is the most insidious form of blockage to speed and action. Passive resistance, if unchecked, can fatally damage the delivery of any project or strategy, and, I've learned to my cost, must be tackled head-on. *What pockets of "passive resistance" exist in your organization, and what actions are you taking to tackle them head-on?*

If you can tackle these roadblocks head-on, you can rapidly increase the ability of your organization to be both first and the fastest to adapt to changes in your market. Over recent years, I have helped many businesses increase the pace of their growth agenda, but my first experience of a step change in organizational speed happened when I worked for the U.K. retailer, Boots the Chemists, in 2003.

The Critical Role of the "Sprinter-in-Chief": Richard Baker Puts "The Chemists" Back into Boots

Boots the Chemists is a British institution. Established in 1849, when John Boot opened a herbal medicine shop in Nottingham, the initial growth of the business was driven by his son, Jesse Boot, establishing the company's reputation as "Chemist to the Nation." During the 20th century not only did the size of the store chain continue to grow, but Boots had created some of the United Kingdom's leading health and beauty brands, including the skincare brand No7 and the suncare brand, Soltan, and its scientists had also developed the ibuprofen painkiller during the 1960s. By 2003, the U.K. chain had grown to more than 1,500 stores and the company also operated retail stores and implants in other international markets including the United States.

But all was not well within the company. In the United Kingdom, the business faced increasing competitive pressure from the fast-growing grocers, particularly Tesco and Asda, and was losing market share. Although higher margins had improved profits, retail revenues had stalled at just over £4 billion for the best part of a decade. These issues were not unexpected by management and as early as 1989 the company had sought to deliver sustainable growth by buying the Ward White Group in a fiercely fought takeover. Ward White ran a diverse set of retailers, including the Halfords auto parts chain, the Payless do-it-yourself chain, and AG Stanley, the owner of FADS DIY, a home improvement chain. This acquisition was a clear attempt at retail diversification or, a "spray" tactic to find another growth opportunity rather than fixing the core business, and it quickly became clear that it wasn't going to work.

During the 1990s, the company also sought—unsuccessfully—to find profitable growth through international retail expansion. As the U.K. competitive environment intensified, a different leadership team "sprayed" again by creating a new well-being services business to sit alongside the company's retail chain. Although the new business's launch had required significant capital investment, it failed to engage consumers and delivered three years of losses. Steve Russell, the group's CEO since 2000 and a Boots veteran of over 30 years, left the business and a new CEO, Richard Baker, was appointed.

Baker joined Boots from Asda where he had been Chief Operating Officer. Asda, which had been acquired by Wal-Mart in the late 1990s, had grown rapidly for the past decade, and Baker had risen rapidly through the ranks following his recruitment from Mars, the confectionary giant. Baker had a rapid impact on the Boots organization and its trading results. In a little over three years, Baker had returned "top-line growth" to the business, as shown in Figure 2.3, and, equally importantly,

To: Ex-Co

From: Richard Baker

There a few behaviors that I expect from myself and my teams. I thought it might help you, if I provide an initial insight:

Integrity above all else - integrity is how we behave when no one else is watching. It is saying that what you think honestly and openly, with respect for other. It is killing gossip and seeing the good in others. It is admitting to mistakes fast.... good news can wait.

All of us is better than any of us - teamwork is the secret ingredient. We deliver on promises to each other. We put each other's work ahead of our own. We debate in private, and concur in public. We show trust. We talk each other up in the presence of others.

World-class leadership - we are all leaders in the company. We lead with our ears not our mouths. We say thank you and we look for every opportunity to celebrate success. When success occurs we give credit to others. When failure occurs we take responsibility personally. We start and finish meetings on time and we set a stretching example to others at all times. Development of our people is a priority.

We set the pace - no one in the company will work faster than we do. We must demand the impossible, set stretch goals and be unreasonable to the job done. Few people know the limit of their abilities. We will make decisions not defer them. We will encourage brevity and simplicity. Complexity is the enemy of pace. Less is more.

Work, rest and play - while working hard, we will also encourage a balanced approach to life. We will take holidays and encourage those around us to do so. We will take our work seriously but not ourselves. Encourage people to have fun. Laughter is the greatest cure of stress and ill-health. Morale improvement is the first step to productivity improvement.

Figure 2.3 Richard Baker's leadership team memo

had created a more optimistic, growth-focused, and can-do culture across the organization. I know this, because I was there, working as part of the strategy and business development teams.

I met Richard in his spacious office at DFS Limited, the United Kingdom's leading sofa retailer, where he is now the Chairman. We spoke about his appointment at Boots, his priorities throughout his tenure, and some of the issues and barriers he came across. Baker's manner is sociable and conversational, but when he wishes to make a serious point, he fixes you with a steely gaze, as if ramming home his point through sheer will. Throughout our conversation, four factors become evident as the real cornerstones of Baker's leadership style: strategic focus; higher expectations; lean organization; continuous communication.

1. **Strategic Focus.** "My first impression was that Boots no longer stood for anything," explains Baker. "The company was a jack-of-all-trades and was going nowhere. It sold health and beauty products, but it still also stocked pots, pans and even homebrew! Unbelievably, Boots was no longer the market leader in pharmacy prescriptions, and it didn't even have the green pharmacy cross on the outside of the stores. My priority was to refocus the retailer on health and beauty; I wanted to put 'The Chemists' back into Boots." As Baker sorted out his office in the weekend before his first day, he came across a 100-year-old advertisement for the retailer, which read: Boots the Chemists—Biggest, Best, Cheapest, Stores Everywhere. "I realized that the answer was in front of me," said Baker. "It may have been created a century ago, but it summed up perfectly what we needed to do. I shared the advertisement at my very first public briefing the following day, and the five strategic priorities we created for the business a few months later—Healthcare First, Boots For Value, Only At Boots, Right Stores Right Place, and Expert Customer Care—were really only restatements of that sign."

The focus on retail health and beauty led to some immediate growth initiatives. Store opening hours were extended, many pharmacies were kept open until midnight, prices were dropped on everyday toiletries in line with the rest of the market, and greater investment was put into Boots's own brands, particularly No. 7.

Top-line performance responded to this renewed health and beauty focus, reversing the decline of the previous leadership team. Profit performance lagged revenues, as a result of the impact of lower prices on margins, but the sale of noncore assets, including the disposal of the healthcare products business, Boots Healthcare International, to Reckitt Benckiser for $3 billion, created a far leaner pharmacy and retail chain that enabled the subsequent merger with Alliance Unichem, a European pharmacy wholesaler, in 2006. Strategic focus created both speed and growth, or, as Baker put it when we met, "You can't spray and sprint!"

2. **Higher Expectations.** If greater strategic focus was Baker's top priority, higher expectations followed right behind. In fact, he believed that the retailer's constant dabbling in unnecessary adjacencies and its lack of focus reflected its low level of ambition. As Baker said to me, "There's no such thing as ex-growth companies (those with no growth potential), only ex-growth management." On Baker's first day, he shared his expectations with his newly inherited leadership team (see Figure 2.3). The memo focuses on his personal values and his expectation of leadership behaviors, emphasizing a need for higher levels of energy, decisiveness, and action. Baker's initial impression of the wider organization was that the people were generally capable and engaged, but that they were also defeatist, lacking ambition and pace. His immediate task was to reenergize the leadership team. After a few weeks, he let a couple of directors go, in part to send a signal to the organization that there was a need for a leaner business, and over the following few months other directors also left the business.

As Baker built his new team, he didn't generally look outside the company but promoted from within. Insiders including Ian Filby (who would go on to lead DFS, where we were meeting), Rob Fraser (who subsequently became the IT Director of the U.K. grocer, Sainsbury's), and Alex Gourlay (who stayed to lead the Boots's U.K. business after Baker's departure and who became the President of Walgreens USA following Alliance Boots's acquisition by the U.S. pharmacy giant in 2014) became part of the new team to kick-start growth. As Baker told me, "I needed to remove the existing retail director who was a nice guy but I just didn't think he was 'on it.'

Alex [Gourlay] was running an HR project but whenever I met him I thought, 'This guy gets it. He knows how the company works, he's a pharmacist and shopkeeper, and he's likeable. I'm sure he can help get the juices flowing in the company again.'" It was important for Baker to ensure that the knowledge of how the business operated was kept within the organization and the leadership team, but that the leaders needed to lead more actively. To this end, Baker reintroduced more formal office clothing, as a signal that the executive team was playing to win, and he also appointed Scott Wheway from Tesco to step change operational performance across the store chain.

3. **Lean Organization.** When Baker was Chief Operating Officer at Asda, the head office employed around 800 colleagues. On his arrival at Boots, over 3,000 people worked at Baker's new headquarters. In spite of the resistance he received from several other members of the leadership team he inherited (several of whom would later leave the business), Baker drove through a plan to reduce the head office size to no more than 2,000 people. He believed that fewer people would help to improve the pace and energy of the organization. "What do you see when you walk around a head office?" he asked me. "Most of the time you see people tapping on their PC keyboards, and they tend to be replying to emails they receive from their colleagues. There is no extra productivity; in fact it destroys productivity. If four people meet for 30 minutes to decide on an issue, it takes a total of two work hours to make the decision. If eight people are invited to the meeting, that same decision will take far longer to make. If it takes half an hour for four people, for instance, it can easily take two hours, or 16 work hours, to make that very same decision. The decision is no better, but it takes eight times more work hours. And this was happening right across the business."

A little over three months into his role, Baker made the announcement to a public meeting of the entire head office. Visibly backed by his chairman, Nigel Rudd, Baker was admittedly tense before the briefing. At the end of his announcement, and to his surprise, there was polite applause. "There wasn't any cheering or hollering," admitted Baker. "But there was a round of applause. It was clear that the troops' understanding of the situation and what was required was better than many of my generals.'" Baker aimed to complete the process as quickly as possible and, as the changes were made, head office staff satisfaction, engagement, and morale scores actually improved rather than fell.

4. **Continuous Communication.** Baker's personal updates to the head office team became a regular feature of his time at Boots. In these sessions, as well as his personal interactions with people from across the business, he would remain upbeat, and focus on how the five strategic priorities were continuing to deliver. His relentless repetition of the new strategy meant that people quickly understood it and were able to cite the priorities in their own meetings. Critically, however, Baker didn't limit his communication to dry statistics, but also focused on stories that brought the new strategy and focus to life. Baker and Gourlay decided to have a stores conference where every store manager would attend, the first time this had happened in living memory. The very idea of a conference attended by all the store managers—most of them also the store's main pharmacist—had been previously discounted by the executive team on the basis that there weren't enough locums in the country to backfill the loss of the pharmacy managers and that, even if they could, the cost would be too great to justify the event. In other words, simply running the conference sent a clear signal of intent to the entire organization.

Baker wanted to make sure that his set-piece session highlighted the critical work of the store teams through a series of stories, rather than giving a more formal PowerPoint lecture. Following the bombing of Omagh's retail high street in 1998 in which 29 people died, for example, the manager of the town's store had kept the shop open and supported the victims and their families throughout that terrible weekend. The store team had not previously received any public recognition from the company and Baker was determined to address this issue, and for other store teams where managers and colleagues had gone out of their way to do the right thing. "I wanted our store managers to know that they were our heroes," explained Baker. "The conference was a physical demonstration that we were relying on them to lead our recovery, and it was vital throughout the turnaround of the business that we kept them up to speed with our performance, our issues and our successes, and that we genuinely listened to and acted on both their concerns and their ideas."

Richard Baker's time wasn't plain sailing in any way. The business struggled to grow profits and the culture, despite its improvements, was still relatively conservative. Baker himself gives his own tenure a score of "maybe six or seven out of ten." Critically, however, the company's core revenues grew as did its share of the U.K. pharmacy, consumer healthcare, and beauty retail markets. What's more, following the disposal of Boots Healthcare International, the business was completely focused on retail pharmacy and health and beauty. The merger with Alliance Unichem in 2006—the point at which Baker left the business—completed the circle of Baker's aim of returning the business back to its roots. Alliance Unichem was a European pharmacy wholesaler, but it also ran 1,000 pharmacies both in the United Kingdom and overseas. The greater buying power of the new group, called Alliance Boots, and its pharmacy focus delivered a 21st-century twist of Jesse Boot's 19th-century vision. The subsequent acquisition of the group by KKR in 2008 and its 2015 sale to Walgreen's, the U.S. drugstore giant, took that vision onto a truly global stage. Above all, however, Baker had re-set the ambition, energy, and focus of the organization. As he had promised the business on his very first day, he had put "The Chemists" back into Boots.

CHAPTER 3

Organizing for Speed and Agility

The Power of Simplicity in a Complex World

William of Ockham was a 14th-century English Franciscan friar who became famous as a logician and theologian. He was an influential thinker of his time, but we know him now primarily as a result of Ockham's Razor, which was his key principle to problem solving. Ockham's Razor states, "plurality should not be posited without necessity," but it's probably easier to think of it as this: "All things being equal the best solution is probably the simplest." In other words, even though a more complex solution may ultimately be found to be superior, if in doubt err on the side of simplicity. Ockham's Razor has served scientists and philosophers well throughout the subsequent centuries, acting as a useful rule of thumb in the development of new theories and models.

The concept of Ockham's Razor is equally relevant to organizational design. If in doubt, choose the simplest option. I know that the world is complex and that the digital technology revolution, globalization, and higher levels of competition are all drivers of greater organizational complexity, but it is incumbent on you to find the simplest solution possible if you want your company to move at pace. Even in multiproduct, multichannel, multicustomer, and multigeography businesses, where complexity lurks around every corner, you must your focus on simplicity. I'm not saying that your organization must be simple, but it must be as simple as it possibly can while still delivering your strategy.

	SIMPLICITY STATEMENT	SCALE OF AGREEMENT
1	We have a clear strategic intent that, in simple, every day terms, articulates how we will succeed	0% 100%
2	As a management team we have identified a handful of objectives (3-6) that drive our focus and activity	0% 100%
3	We have an over-arching #1 goal that is the ultimate driver of our decisions	0% 100%
4	We have crystal-clear accountabilities across the business and managers are never concerned that they're stepping on someone else's toes	0% 100%
5	We have minimized the number of management layers – there is no further room for improvement	0% 100%
6	Managers know exactly how to seek approval for a major decision or investment	0% 100%
7	Our planning process is short, sharp and effective, taking only a few weeks to complete	0% 100%
8	When an initiative or business activity isn't working it is quickly improved or killed – we do not allow problems to fester	0% 100%
9	We miminize the number of formal meetings and senior managers' time is focused on delivering a great customer experience	0% 100%
10	This is not a political organization. Everyone feels free to have their say, and we all feel as if we're on the same side	0% 100%

Figure 3.1 The simplicity test

As we saw in Chapter 2 and Richard Baker's tenure as the CEO of Boots the Chemists, the creation of a "lean" organization at that U.K. retailer not only enabled faster decision making and more rapid actions, it also improved the morale of the people that worked there. Greater simplicity led to greater speed.

Figure 3.1 gives you 10 questions to determine the level of simplicity in your own organization. There is no one perfect organizational solution—each and every company has its own unique set of circumstances, needs, and priorities—but The Simplicity Test does highlight four underlying principles that enable the development of organizations that are fast, agile, and decisive:

1. **Deliver Instantaneous Accountability.** An organization that moves quickly to meet new opportunities, and which can improve and innovate faster than its competitors, can only do so when managers and teams feel in control of their own destiny. If they are always waiting for a starting gun to be fired before sprinting, they are likely to be the last ones off the blocks. It's even worse where there are too many managers in the organization with insufficiently defined objectives and responsibilities. In those cases, the starting gun only leads to people looking at each other to work out who's meant to go first.

   Managers will only take the initiative if they honestly believe that it is in their best interests to do so. That means that they must first believe that their organization, and more specifically their line manager, wants them to take responsibility and make things happen. For that to happen, they need the space, the elbow room to move and act without feeling they are treading on another manager's toes, which is why pace is so closely correlated with fewer, not more, layers of management. As I discussed above, it is possible for a "command and control" style organization to be fast-paced, but only if the "commander" has a detailed knowledge of the whole business, is continuously available to make calls as they arise, and has the willingness to make fast decisions. Otherwise, as the British army saying goes, it is a case of "hurry up and wait!"

2. **Create Broader Spans of Control.** It's hard to move when you're in a straitjacket. Similarly, it's hard to drive and deliver change when you only have a very narrow area of control and limited headroom to make decisions. At one of my clients, the CEO, driven by pressure on his costs, reduced his number of senior managers from around 200 to less than 100. He expected that the remaining managers would deliver less than before and that the company would struggle to execute its major initiatives. To his surprise and delight, he was wrong on both counts. The senior managers' newfound freedom led them to take the necessary decisions more quickly and move things forward faster than they had achieved before. They didn't need to

wait for a perfect situation before pressing the button, and as they no longer needed to ask permission from peers who previously would have had their own related agenda for change, they were simply able to make things happen once a solution had been found.

3. **Focus on the Quality, Not Quantity of People.** If you're going to have fewer managers and fewer people than feels comfortable to deliver your full agenda, you will need to make sure that your people have the ability and desire to deliver. For example, after the appointment of a new retail director, one of my clients changed over 50 percent of its retail staff within 12 months. The new director only wanted people with the right attitudes, behaviors, and capabilities in place to deliver a radical new growth strategy. The new strategy transformed the retail channel's performance within that year. The revenue and profit growth was not delivered entirely smoothly—there were many issues and emergencies to resolve—but the transformation would have been impossible to deliver, and never at the pace at which it succeeded, without first ensuring that the stores and supporting teams were staffed with people of the right quality.

4. **Align Individual and Organizational Goals.** Real pace and sustained performance growth can only happen in companies where your people are committed to your success, not merely compliant. That only happens when people feel that is in their best self-interest to pursue the same goals and objectives as the ones that you have set. We will discuss the importance of creating a culture where people are genuinely involved in the organization's mission and success in the next chapter, but a critical starting point is aligning each individual's objectives with the organization's most important goals. It is a simple thing for the leadership team to get right, but all too often managers set their people goals that are at best tangential, and in some cases, antithetical to the business's most important performance targets.

But it can be done. For example, at Bristan, a U.K. faucet and shower business, the executive team meticulously drive down their corporate objectives into team and individual objectives through their "goal deployment" system. People don't have the same goal, but they do have operational goals that directly drive their #1 performance goal. Similarly, at U.K. sofa retailer DFS (which we will visit in much more detail in Chapter 7), virtually all employees have a personal goal that is directly driven by the company's top priority of growing customers satisfaction and they are rewarded for their contribution to its improvement through a generous corporate bonus scheme. In both these businesses, having established personal goals that clearly drive the companies' priorities, senior managers spend less time on ensuring compliance to a plan and more of their time working with their teams to find new ways to accelerate performance improvement. The question for you is what are the most important performance goals for your business, and what steps have you taken to ensure that these goals are directly manifested in the performance goals of your people? After all, if you're not setting out to reward people for their own particular role in achieving your top priorities, you shouldn't be surprised if you never achieve them.

Destroying Silos, Accelerating Growth

Perhaps nothing prevents businesses achieving their goals at pace than the existence of functional and departmental silos. In some businesses, the political environment encourages some leaders to pursue their own objectives ahead of the company's priorities, but silos also exist in more benign environments. All functional teams will have their own priorities, so if you fail to find effective ways to overcome the inherent barriers that exist in any organizational structure, you will always fail to achieve your ability to rapidly change, develop, and grow your business in line with your markets.

In Stephen Elop's Nokia memo, he complained that the business had failed to collaborate internally. The company was obviously pursuing a range of strategic initiatives—such as Symbian and MeeGo—but had been unable to find a way to integrate these programs into coherent and focused cross-functional developments that everyone could support and get behind. As Elop found out to Nokia's cost, collaboration and the removal of organizational silos does not happen without active and disciplined leadership. Here are 12 ways you can remove silos and accelerate action and growth in your organization.

1. **Build a Leadership *Team*.** The emphasis here is on the word *team*. Top talent is the starting point, not end point of an effective

leadership team. More than that, it is the job of the CEO to clarify executive accountabilities, develop a sense of shared purpose, support and encourage honest communication and trust between the team members, and develop a strategy and leadership agenda that demands cross-functional behaviors. Without a fully functioning team, executive members tend to come together like a UN assembly meeting: each executive will have his or her own independent priorities and agenda, discussions are rarely focused on common goals, decision making is protracted and unclear, and, as a result, the organization is slow at getting anything done.

At one of my clients, for instance, there had been years of mutual antipathy and mistrust between successive Commercial Directors and Marketing Directors. Consequently, each function pursued its own agenda almost irrespective of the other's priorities. A newly appointed CEO decided to address the issue, however, and promoted two new directors on the basis of their existing working relationship. The pair's mutual trust and respect led to joint initiatives and strategies, and created an environment where their teams were willing to cooperate on new, emerging ideas. Within a few months of the new directors' appointment, a new customer strategy and plan had been agreed, compared to the previous five years where no real change in customer focus had been possible.

2. **Have Everyone Focused on the Same Goal.** The more that the entire organization are pursuing the same goal, the greater the chance that you will remove functional silos and build a single organizational community. Conversely, if you break down your #1 goal into functional and departmental goals, you will increase the probability of different priorities across your different functions. At one of my manufacturing clients, for example, all the departments' goals are focused on delivering the company's #1 goal of achieving sales of 15,000 units per week. As the CEO observed, one of the side effects of this move has been to step change the level of interaction and integration between manufacturing, sales, and marketing so that issues are resolved more quickly and new ideas that can help the company achieve its goal faster are developed more rapidly than happened in the past.

3. **Pursue a "Monofocused" Agenda.** I once led a consulting project for a U.K. homewares retailer, to identify new priorities for growth. To be honest, I had hedged my bets by proposing three different opportunities that the business should develop and test. The CEO listened politely to my recommendations before saying, "There's only one of these opportunities that I want to pursue. It's far bigger than the other ideas, it fits best with who we are, and we know how to pull it off. We need to focus on this one so that we can really get going." The atmosphere in the meeting was instantly transformed. The other executives and managers immediately started discussing how they could work together to develop an initial prototype as well as how they could bring the ideas into some of the new stores they would soon be opening. As a consultant, I learned my lesson. I now make sure that my recommendations are precise and focused—"monofocused" is perhaps a better word—enabling my clients to deliver more quickly and with greater integration and alignment across their various functions.

4. **Reward Cross-Functional Behavior.** Most managers and employees aren't naturally disposed to supporting and perpetuating functional silos. But they are naturally disposed to acting in their own rational self-interest. In other words, your teams will act in line with how they are rewarded. If you want your managers and colleagues to operate on a cross-functional basis, you must reward their cross-functional behaviors. For the past two decades, GE staff have been assessed and rewarded on the basis of a 9-box square where everyone is assessed on two dimensions: results and behaviors. In other words, behaviors are seen to be as important as results when it comes to the annual bonus, and only those managers who perform effectively on both dimensions are promoted to more senior levels.

5. **Avoid Functionally Led Rewards.** The quid pro quo of rewarding cross-functional behaviors is to remove any functionally focused rewards. At the start of each year, critically review each department's objectives and bonus targets and ensure that they can be directly linked to your business goals and can only be achieved if the function works effectively with other business functions. In most organizations, the departmental targets are set such that they are under the total control of the departmental leader, but in my experience,

greater levels of organizational alignment, speed, and effectiveness occur when each functional team can only achieve their full reward if they can work effectively with other functions and departments. It's a case of "you scratch my back and I'll scratch yours" and it helps to build a single, integrated community and accelerates growth.

6. **Embed Cross-Functional Career Development.** Traditional career development has been largely "straight line." People start in a particular function, say marketing, and may take on a variety of marketing roles, but are fundamentally promoted through the hierarchy without gaining experience in other functions, for example sales or operations. This career development approach establishes deep technical experience but it fails to create multidimensional managers and can lead to senior managers thinking through a functional lens, rather than adopting a wider business standpoint. Cross-functional career development eradicates these limitations, enabling your managers to assess and address issues and opportunities from a variety of perspectives, ensuring that they act in the best interest of your customers and the business as a whole.

7. **Use Cross-Business Mentors.** Line managers are the starting point for developing cross-functional skills and behaviors, but relying solely on a silo-led system to minimize the negative effects of silo behaviors is unlikely to be sufficient. Using mentors to provide independent and confidential feedback to aspiring managers and colleagues is a further way to embed effective cross-functional behaviors. All of your leaders should, at any one time, be mentoring a number of people in the organization, and these "mentees" should ideally include a majority who work in functions different to that led by the mentor. That way, your managers can start to better understand the perspectives and demands of different departments and identify ways to effectively influence and build alignment with managers from other departments.

8. **Promote Process-Led Performance Improvement Programs.** Just as GE has led the way on rewarding cross-functional behaviors, the company also famously created, or at least highlighted, the concept of "Workout" projects: initiatives that focused on resolving process issues that required a cross-functional team of frontline colleagues to rapidly identify, agree, and recommend the best way forward. The

idea of "workout" teams may not be new, but they are still a valuable way to destroy silos in 21st-century organizations. Not only can "workout" projects deliver rapid improvements to issues that cannot be solved within functions, but they also build the relationships and trust between people who may otherwise only have marginal contact with each other. In my experience of leading similar projects and programs, involvement in a two-day workout initiative can establish the bonds that enable people who work on the same process, but in different functions, to call each other directly to sort out future issues when, in the past, they would have simply blamed each other and gone through their line managers to raise problems.

9. **Establish Three-Dimensional Feedback.** Many businesses now look to gain feedback from line managers, departmental colleagues, and members of a manager's own team when assessing performance. But it is possible to move outside of a single function in this process and to provide more three-dimensional feedback. Identifying critical colleagues in other departments, external suppliers and partners and even specific customers, can give richer and even more valuable feedback as to how well an individual has worked at pace across organizational boundaries to deliver results for customers and the company. At one major corporation, for instance, I was asked, as an external consultant, to provide formal feedback on several managers and their effectiveness as part of a major corporate project we had worked on together. I was able to provide feedback on each manager's level of active involvement in the project, their contribution to the solutions we developed, and their ability to act and work in a cross-functional manner for the wider benefit of the business, giving each line manager insights that they wouldn't normally have had in a traditional performance assessment review.

10. **Colocate Program and Process Teams.** Wherever possible, physically colocate and bring your cross-functional program and process teams together. Colocation enables far better communication and builds the trust and relationships that are critical to the success of your most important initiatives and activities. At one of my clients, the development of a new customer strategy and related projects involved senior managers from the commercial, sales, finance, and operations teams. In the early stages, these managers came together

one day a week and, to be honest, the team's progress was relatively slow. It was only when each manager began to work full-time on the project, and was physically brought together into a project team zone in the head office that was situated next to the executive offices, that the speed and effectiveness of the work began to deliver against our ambitious timescales. The managers no longer felt like they were representing their own particular function at these weekly sessions, but became, instead, completely focused on delivering the best possible results for the company and its customers in the fastest possible time.

11. **Celebrate Victories Together.** Communities come together to celebrate success. They don't do this in individual functions and silos, but as a single group. Wal-Mart has consistently created a unique and compelling culture and sense of community, and a key enabler of that culture has been its annual shareholder meeting. Unlike most corporations, where this meeting is a dry, financially-focused session and where the CEO's main hope is that it passes unnoticed by the wider world, the Wal-Mart review has become a week-long extravaganza where colleagues from across the globe come together to play sports, attend parties, and have the chance to watch some of the world's biggest entertainers—the 2014 meeting included performances from Pharrell Williams and Harry Connick Jr., among others, for instance. The financial results are not always, of course, what the company's executive team may have wished for, but the shareholders' meeting is seen as a chance to promote the corporations values, highlight customer successes, and celebrate the organization's unsung heroes.

12. **Remove "Silo Imperialists."** The first 11 actions I have recommended are all positive steps to build community and create and embed cross-functional behaviors across your organization. The final action is, perhaps, more negative, but it is a vital step if you are to succeed in destroying your functional silos. I have already mentioned that most managers aren't naturally bent on developing and perpetuating functional silos—but some managers are! These managers crave control and power above everything else, even when it is the detriment to the wider organization's success, and they must be removed from the organization if they are unwilling or unable to change.

Decision Making on the Run

In the first chapter, I set out a summary of the decline and fall of the Nokia cell phones business. At the heart of Nokia's destruction was a failure of decision making at the highest levels in the company. From 2006 onwards, faced with new, dynamic competition and unprecedented levels of technological innovation, Nokia's leaders were unable to make the timely, effective decisions necessary for the company's survival, let alone its success. Part of the problem lay in the complexity of the Nokia organization, part lay in the arrogance and inertia of senior manager mind-sets, and, as we've just discussed, part lay in the creation of functional silos that created camps that favored one technological approach over another and hindered effective cross-functional cooperation.

The result of these organizational and cultural issues was a dearth of strategic decisions that could possibly save the business. The board held onto the company's historic strategy and sources of success for too long and, by the time Elop had articulated the issues, the tide of competition and consumer choice had long turned against Nokia, and even the radical choices Elop made were unable to save the business. So, how do you ensure that you are able to make effective operational and, more importantly, strategic decisions in fast-paced, turbulent markets? How do you establish the systems and protocols for decision making on the run? As Figure 3.2 shows, there are three core principles you need in place to enable you to make rapid, timely decisions in dynamic and uncertain environments.

Factor #1: Goal Clarity

In reality, there are only two types of decision. The first is about setting a goal, an objective or destination. This decision sets the direction and compass for the business, helping everyone understand what success looks like and the fewer goals you have the easier this is to do. The second type of decision is centered on finding the best way to achieve your goal and objective. The key question you need to answer is which

Figure 3.2 Three factors for fast-paced decision making

of the options you have developed help you reach your goal in the fastest and most cost-effective way, within whatever risk constraints you have established.

Most decisions managers take are the second type. They are all about working out the best way to achieve the goal. If you have failed to set a clear destination for your organization or you have too many, potentially conflicting goals, it becomes impossible for managers to easily work out which options and opportunities they should be pursuing and which they should be ignoring. Elop's note suggests that the company suffered from a lack of direction; there was no guiding compass that could help managers make appropriate, consistent, and mutually supportive decisions across the organization.

We will talk more in Chapter 4 about the importance of having only a handful of corporate goals and also identifying your #1 goal that sits above all your other targets. In companies where I have worked with the executive team to clarify the #1 goal, managers have repeatedly commented how it helps make subsequent investment decisions far easier and far faster. In these organizations, managers only really need to answer one simple question to enable them to take the decision: will this idea help us achieve our #1 goal at an acceptable cost and risk?

How well do your managers understand your key objectives and your #1 goal, and how often are their decisions directly based on achieving them?

Factor #2: Unambiguous Accountability

Individuals make virtually all business decisions. In all my time as a strategy director, I can only think of one decision that was the result of a collective executive vote. Even if these individual decision makers ask for information from others, seek out colleagues for their views or pull together a committee to help them make the best decision possible; in the end, an individual will make the call. Given this fact, it seems remarkable that so few organizations have worked out precisely which individual is accountable for which decisions. All too often, decision rights are inferred, or there is an unspoken search for consensus, creating confusion, frustration, and delay in equal measure.

For example, the CEO of an IT services business I worked with once decided that the executive team should collectively agree the company's annual operating plan. While he would chair the meetings, he wanted full agreement on targets, resource allocation, and operating plans from the executive team. Three months into the process, the following year's performance targets had still not been set. Middle managers and frontline teams became frustrated with the lack of progress and their faith in the leadership team of a business that was already struggling to compete effectively was further undermined by the lack of clarity. In the end, the COO and CFO came together to drive through some initial decisions, but it was less than surprising that the CEO was removed less than a year later.

How clear are your decision-making accountabilities, and how well communicated are they across your organization?

Factor #3: Commercial Judgment

In dynamic, fast-paced markets, it is not always possible to have a full analysis of the situation before making decisions, and when you are looking to innovate and lead your competitors, you are unlikely to have any precedents available to help you make your decisions. So, despite the rise in "big data" and the almost incomprehensible computing power and analytical capabilities that are freely available to all companies, it is more important than ever that you and your colleagues can demonstrate effective commercial judgment. By this I don't mean experience, although that can be an important component. Instead, commercial judgment is all about applied wisdom, where you can intuitively identify what is likely to work and what isn't, where you have the self-confidence and self-esteem to trust your judgment, and where you also have the "street smarts" to find a route to success that your colleagues will support and deliver.

How strong is your commercial judgment, and that of your colleagues, and how often do you trust it sufficiently to make quicker, more effective decisions?

Critically, rapid, effective decision making on the run doesn't need just one or two of these factors; all three need to be present if you are to succeed. As shown in Figure 3.2, even where two of the factors exist you will still fail. Here are the four possible positions:

1. **Swampland.** In this situation, you have the individual and collective judgment and also have a clear goal. However, you don't have clear decision-making accountabilities and, as a result, decisions become stuck in an organizational swamp or bog of discussion, debate, and hesitation. As with the IT Services, company's planning process, a "swampland" situation generates huge amounts of frustration across an organization while everyone waits for "them" to sort things out.

2. **Blunderland.** You may have a clear goal and unambiguous accountabilities, but without commercial judgment you will make too many poor decisions. There are two main types of errors in this situation. The first is that you simply shoot from the hip and make poor commercial decisions. The second type of error is one of omission, and takes place when you fail to make a decision. Your uncertainty, your

need for greater analysis, and an excessive aversion to risk means that you avoid making important decisions however critical they may be. This appears to have been one of the key underlying issues at Nokia where potential decisions that were vital to the future success and survival of the business were put on the "too difficult" pile for far too long.

3. **Driftland.** Here, you have good commercial judgment and effective accountabilities, but lack a clear goal. As a result, managers and executives make the best decisions they can, but they often fail to take the business in a single, focused direction. The cumulative effect of these decisions is that the company may achieve some incremental gains, but often fails to deliver the major step changes required or seize the biggest opportunities in their market. Unwittingly, as we have already discussed, the absence of an overarching company goal creates a situation where divisions and functions establish their own, independent goals, creating fertile conditions for organizational silos.

4. **The United States of Decisiveness.** It is only in this situation that your company will really move at pace and have a chance of leading its market. This means that your job as a leader of your business is to establish and communicate a clear goal for the organization, ensure people know their own and others' decision rights, and that you hire and develop managers with effective commercial judgment. If you can do these three tasks effectively, you will transform the capacity of your company to move at pace and become your market's leading player. All of the successful businesses I have worked with have worked on each of these three critical factors and found ways to accelerate the pace of decision making. Some of these businesses were highly centralized, where most decisions were still taken by the most senior people, whereas others had far greater levels of delegation, but in all fast-paced businesses, management has worked out an effective way to make decisions on the run. If you fail to find a way to speed up your decision making, you will never be able to lead your markets, but once you do implement faster decision-making processes, almost anything is possible.

Turning Your Organization on a Dime

It is evident that the challenge for any executive team in driving ongo-ing change and creating an organization that is capable and willing to continuously evolve is massive. Consistently turning your organization on a dime is possible, however. My favorite example is the U.K. electrical retailer, Dixons. Founded in the 1930s, the company has become a pan-European market leader, and has included brands such as Dixons, Currys, The Link, PC World, Electro World, and Elkøp in its portfolio. The busi-ness operates in a notoriously challenging market and in recent years has faced fierce competition in the United Kingdom from established rivals such as Comet, Richer Sounds and John Lewis, the relentless rise of low-price Internet retailers, led by Amazon, and the market entrants including the U.S. giant, Best Buy.

Dixons—now part of Carphone Dixons following a 2014 merger with Carphone Warehouse—hasn't always succeeded with its changes and has suffered loss-making years, but I admire the business because it has never stopped trying to evolve in line with its market. In terms of the three foundation fundamentals, the business has been organized into two distinct areas. First, it has its customer-facing formats, each with their own management teams. Second, it has an integrated back-office opera-tion covering buying, logistics, and IT. This structure has created simplic-ity and clarity for the entire organization, providing the format teams with full accountability for trading performance, embedding integrated operational support that reduces the development of silos that inhibit the pace of other multifascia, international retailers.

In addition, the company's unambiguous accountabilities have given managers and leaders the ability to make rapid decisions at both an op-erational and strategic level. Here are two examples:

1. In the 1990s, the leadership team decided to create a cell/mobile phone shop chain called The Link. In the early years, The Link grew rapidly, but as the market evolved and the competition, led by the main networks of Vodafone, O2, Orange and T-Mobile, intensified, it was sold to O2 (who had previously owned 40 percent of the chain) a little over 10 years after its launch. In other words, Dixon's

management had been decisive both in entering and also exiting a new business opportunity.

2. Following the acquisition of four stores in 1993, PC World was run independently of the group's other formats. Back in the 1990s, the buyers of PCs were a relatively small niche of the buyers of TVs and other electrical equipment, and there was little overlap between the role of a TV and that of a PC to consumers. Over time, however, the interplay between TVs and PCs has increased markedly and they now form two elements of a much bigger digital market. As a result, PC World and Currys were fully integrated in 2010 in jointly branded stores and the remaining PC World stores were shut. In the new, integrated stores, the PC World brand highlights the group's PC credentials, but integrating the offer into the wider electrical store enables shoppers to buy across the group's full range of digital products. Again, Dixon's management made clear, positive decisions, first to enter the PC retail market and second to close the stand-alone stores to better meet the shifting consumer demands and ongoing product innovation.

This courage to take prudent risks at all stages of a business's lifecycle underpins much of Dixon's corporate history and is highlighted by its 2014 merger with Carphone Warehouse, the United Kingdom's leading independent cell/mobile phone store. Rather than trying to persevere independently, as rivals such as Comet had tried and ultimately failed to do, management recognized that the only way to succeed in the future was to create a large-scale, integrated business. This decision and the subsequent corporate merger also highlights how Dixon's management continues to demonstrate the application of the following four agility building blocks, which has consistently enabled the organization to turn on a dime:

1. **Proactive, Entrepreneurial Leadership.** Turning your organization on a dime is a huge change management task. It cannot be achieved by "remote control" but needs proactive, direct leadership to succeed. A compelling vision, relentless and engaging communication, and visible decisions and actions that support the future direction are all prerequisites of support for change across the wider organization.

In addition, leaders who are able to deliver ongoing, rapid change must also be willing to take prudent risks, even if it means that some failures will result. Throughout its history, Dixons has been led by proactive leaders hungry to develop the business and deliver new, innovative offers. From Stanley Kalms, the son of the group's founder who joined the business at the age of 16, through to John Clare and, following the merger with Carphone Warehouse, Charles Dunstone, executives who err on the side of entrepreneurialism, rather than staid corporate management, have led the group.

2. **Top Talent, Fully Engaged.** Leadership alone is insufficient to deliver consistent success in dynamic markets. Only "A" players who feel full ownership for their decisions and actions can deliver the rapid, consistent organizational change and innovation that's demanded by modern business environments. The organizational approach at Dixons, with clear format and retail ownership for results, is far more likely to attract ambitious talented managers and also develops higher levels of engagement for each business unit's strategy and performance. Following the merger with Carphone Warehouse in 2014, Dixons continued this focus on managing and nurturing a cadre of senior executives and leaders by making early decisions on the future leadership team and implementing a specific retention program for the new organization's top talent.

3. **A Stream of High-Value Options.** Fast-changing markets not only demand ongoing improvement and evolution of your existing products and services, but also the creation of new customer solutions. In fact, it is generally the creation of new business ideas that acts as the internal catalyst for organizational change, and it's only those businesses that are able to create a stream of new, innovative and high-value ideas, trials, start-ups, and acquisitions that generally have the energy and enthusiasm to continuously evolve. Not all your ideas will become commercial successes, so it is vital that you are willing to invest sufficiently in long-term thinking and effective business development processes, but without these ideas and options, managers have no choice but to do their best to preserve the status quo, limiting their company's ability to lead their markets in the future or change as quickly as their markets.

The level of effort you need to put into the development of new growth options will vary from company to company, but one CEO client told me that he aims to focus 80 percent of his time on delivering this year's performance, 15 percent on ensuring success in the following year, and 5 percent focusing on new growth opportunities beyond the next 18 to 24 months, and this seems a reasonable starting point to me. Over the past 20 years, Dixons has consistently developed new business ideas, most famously the creation and sale of Freeserve, the United Kingdom's first free Internet service. More recently, the company developed KnowHow, a team of advisors who are focused on helping customers make the most of their digital products.

4. **Partnering for Pace.** The merger of Dixons and Carphone Warehouse was preceded by a strategic partnership between the two businesses. Most executives now recognize the need to work in partnership with other organizations to develop and deliver faster, more effective innovation, acknowledging that it would simply be too slow and ineffective to build the capability in-house. For decades, partnerships and alliances have underpinned the development of most high-tech businesses, but the trend has become far more widespread as business leaders understand the risks and ultimate futility of trying to do everything in-house. Even the consumer goods giant P&G, for instance, now looks to develop over 50 percent of its new products from ideas sourced outside the business; and idea, which just a few years ago, would have seemed mildly outrageous. There is a difference between recognizing a need to doing something and actually achieving it, however. Partnering to accelerate growth requires a certain set of capabilities and behaviors and can become a source of competitive advantage for businesses. Following the merger of Dixons and Carphone Warehouse, the new company, Dixons Carphone has continued to develop its partnership strategy and in 2015, for example, agreed a trial partnership with Sprint, the U.S. cell network. Under the deal, Dixons Carphone will use their retail capabilities to run 20 Sprint stores, with a view to extending the deal to 500 stores across the United States. From the company's point of view, the potential partnership gives Dixons Carphone low-risk access to the world's largest market and could act as a stepping-stone to further growth opportunities.

The critical point is that fast, responsive, and proactive organizations don't happen by accident. They need to be developed deliberately, and require ongoing focus and management. Keeping your organization "lean" is a good start, but it is not sufficient, on its own, to provide you with the pace and agility required in today's markets. Finally, your organizational approach should reflect your wider business strategy, which is where we'll move next.

CHAPTER 4

Rapid-Fire Strategy

Strategy Ain't What It Used to Be

At the end of a particularly long and grueling strategy meeting with the executive team of a major consumer services business, Alan, the chief executive officer, turned to me and said, "Living quarter by quarter is madness, but in a few years' time people will laugh at us for developing three-year plans." He was right. With the pace of business change today, driven by technology and globalization, long-term plans last about as long as an ice storm in the desert. As military experts put it, plans rarely survive contact with the enemy.

Despite these new realities, many executive teams remain stuck with 20th-century approaches to strategy development. It is still common for companies to take six months or more to develop their new growth strategies. This prolonged, inefficient and largely ineffective approach—involving colossal data analysis projects, the creation of a series of 100-slide decks, and periodic executive meetings where directors are presented with findings and recommendations to comment on—may suit consultants looking to maximize fees, and even some executives who want to look as if they're in control, but it does little to help businesses succeed in fast-changing markets.

Alan was equally right about the madness of "living quarter by quarter." Your business will only be successful if your speed and agility is matched by a clear strategic focus. Pace and flexibility only works if it operates alongside a constant, slow-changing direction. This means that alongside a willingness and commitment to increase pace and jump on and exploit new opportunities as they emerge, you must link this capability with a commitment to a clear and compelling strategic goal. As has always been the case with effective strategies, your rapid, short-term actions must be tied into a longer-term commitment and direction. Speed isn't about jumping on any opportunity; it's about exploiting those opportunities where you have the capability to win and which helps you achieve your longer-term goals.

So, if a strategy looks and feels the same as it always has, and is just as important to corporate success as it was previously, what has changed? What do you now need to do differently to balance the need for organizational pace and agility with the importance of a clear direction? This chapter sets out some practical approaches you can use, but you must first recognize three key principles of strategy management in the 21st century:

1. Big Ideas are More Important than Big Reports

Ever since the publication of Michael Porter's book, *Competitive Strategy*, with its focus on analytical techniques, and the subsequent adoption of his ideas by the major consulting firms, the strategy process has become overwhelmed with excessive analysis and the publication of 100-page slide decks from these strategy "experts." The underlying belief is that if you can understand in more detail what is happening to your business, you will automatically create a better, more compelling direction. This view has some merits—I have undertaken many projects where framing the situation more clearly for management has led to better decisions and an immediate improvement in performance—but it also has some fundamental weaknesses:

- The pace of change in most markets, and the lack of certainty about their future prospects, makes it extremely difficult to analyze with confidence what will really be happening a year or two down the line.
- The analytical reports tend to be undertaken by people who aren't on the executive team; often by consultants external to the organization. This creates a lack of ownership of the thinking by the company's leaders. They become spectators and commentators to the analysis, like members of a sports commentary team, rather than players or coaches on the field of play. As a result, actions and results are diluted.

- The emerging strategy tends to be a relatively safe, "me-too" version of what's already succeeding. Consultants are under constant pressure to demonstrate their expertise and share what's working elsewhere. This pressure, and resulting conservatism, inevitably leads to strategies that are already proven. They may have some clear merits but they will not create true competitive distinctiveness.

The biggest weakness of the analytical approach is that strategies don't automatically result from analysis. In my experience, all great strategies start with an idea. Some analysis may help that idea creation, but intuition and creativity have a much bigger part to play. The creation of Southwest Airlines, Starbucks and FedEx, for instance, all have some analytical logic to their success, but they were all the result of a creatively commercial idea from their owner or executive leader.

2. Be Fixed On the Vision, But Flexible On the Journey

I've always thought that the term *strategic planning* was an oxymoron, but, as a ritual, three-year plans are about as effective to 21st-century business success as wassailing has been to English apple production. Each may make the people involved feel that they have more control over the end results, but the reality is that their performance will actually depend on how they react to the stream of unexpected and unplanned events that will inevitably take place, rather than the effort and energy they put into these up-front activities. The saying "fail to plan and you plan to fail" should be changed to "fail to learn and you learn to fail."

You cannot therefore set out a long-term plan as if you're planning a car journey on the national freeways. There is no satellite navigation that will tell you which exits to take, there are no lanes you should stay within, and there is not even a road ahead that shows you the way—and if there is, then you're probably just copying one of your rivals and, more than likely, in a difficult competitive position. Instead, it is better to think of strategy implementation as a sailing adventure across the sea. You may know your destination, you will probably have made sure that you have sufficient skills and resources for the journey ahead and you will have an idea of the route you need to take, but your actual speed, journey, and success will be driven by how well you react to the constantly shifting winds, the ever-changing currents, and the rise and fall of the tides.

It's the strength and suitability of the boat and its crew, rather than the quality of the initial plan that will determine the speed at which the boat travels. As with sailing, the quickest route to strategic success is rarely a straight line, but is, instead, a zigzag of constant adjustments to environmental conditions, combined with more dramatic turns and detours to avoid major storms and to take advantage of changes in the prevailing winds and currents. It's not a "road map" that you need to deliver your strategy, but a "nautical chart."

In August 2013, for example, Amazon acquired *The Washington Post*. Following the acquisition, Jeff Bezos, the founder and chief executive of Amazon, wrote to the staff of *The Post* about the purchase and what they could expect. In that letter, Bezos wrote: "There is no map, and charting a path ahead will not be easy. We will need to invent, which means we will need to experiment. Our touchstone will be readers, understanding what they care about—government, local leaders, restaurant openings, scout troops, businesses, charities, governors, sports—and working backwards from there. I'm excited and optimistic about the opportunity for invention."[1] Bezos's words echo his approach to long-term planning at Amazon where he once said that the company was "fixed on the vision, flexible on the journey."

3. Remember: Nothing Fails Like Success

The simple answer is that, as a result of the forces we set out in Chapter 1, these advantages are now much more transitory. In Porter's books, he talked about sustainable competitive advantages; that is, advantages that deliver long-term benefits to a business. Coca-Cola's brand recognition, for instance, has delivered a long-term benefit to the company and is still a sustainable competitive advantage for the business. There are other examples, too, of course. Strong, powerful brands have delivered decades of benefits for companies including McDonalds, Tide, Mars, and Kraft.

---

[1]As reported in *The Washington Post*, August 5, 2013.

Similarly, access to huge oil and gas reserves, as well as specific oil exploration, drilling and supply capabilities, has helped ExxonMobil, BP and Royal Dutch Shell, as well as state-backed players such as PetroChina, Gazprom, Saudi Aramco, to continue to dominate the world's energy market. The assets and capabilities that are owned by these corporate giants are a major barrier to effective competition from other potential players; a classic source of sustainable competitive advantage as set out by Porter.

There are many more examples, however, where competitive advantages have become far more transitory. For example, Apple's grip on the tablet market has been significantly weakened since it launched the iPad in 2010. In its first year, the iPad delivered a share of around 80 percent of total market volume, but the growth of Android alternatives, led by Samsung, has meant that while the market has continued to grow to around 50 million units per quarter, Apple's sales have remained stuck at around 10 million units, which in 2013 represented a 20 percent share of the market. The technology and design, which created the iPad's initial surge in demand, has not been sufficiently differentiated to enable the company to maintain a clear lead, and rival tablets have caught up with and now match, if not outperform the iPad across many features.

One of the reasons that these advantages decline so rapidly is the sheer scale of competition. Over 100 rival tablets were released onto the market in the 12 months following the iPad's launch. While many of these new products were complete failures commercially—even the computer giant HP had to slash the price of its initial model to gain any consumer interest—some of the models started to meet the needs of different customer groups and offered features that were more appealing. Samsung, for instance, offered smaller-sized tablets, and Amazon's Kindle Fire offered a much lower purchase price as Amazon sought to make money by selling books and other services rather than generating profits directly from the tablet itself. Over time, this meant that Apple's initial advantages were reduced and its share consequently fell.

The 3Rs of Strategy

Here is my definition of a business strategy: *a framework for guiding decisions and actions across an organization to deliver superior performance.* It's not a plan; instead, it's a formula for future success, and while academics and consultants have persuaded many executives that strategy development is a highbrow activity that only the top 1 percent of intellects can manage, there are really only four factors you need to focus on, as shown in Figure 4.1, The Strategy Arrow:

1. **Your #1 Goal.** This is the specific goal, above all others, that sets out what success actually means for your organization. All businesses have many targets, goals and objectives, but this leads to a lack of clarity. Establishing a goal that sits over and above all your other targets will give you and your team better focus, aids communication across your organization, and helps simplify and accelerate many of your major resource allocation and investment decisions. In fact, I would argue that identifying your #1 goal is the most important strategic decision you will make. The United Kingdom's leading ceramic wall and floor tile retailer, Topps Tiles, for instance, established a #1 goal to grow its market share from 25 percent to 33 percent within five years. As a result, the company developed new service standards, developed new innovative ranges, spent more time attracting trade customers

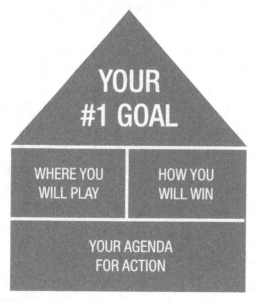

Figure 4.1 The strategy arrow

and developed new formats, specifically to deliver against the goal. As Matt Williams, the CEO said, "The goal galvanized our organization and has been a key part of our success."

2. **Where You Play.** This is the scope of your business, setting out where you have chosen to participate, and includes your target customers, your products and services, your geographical reach, and your channels to market. Most strategic moves are a change in where companies play, both for good and bad. Microsoft's decision to move into the gaming market, through the development of the Xbox, for instance, is an example of change in strategic scope. The company brought its brand, capabilities, and market reach to enter an entirely new market, providing a new platform for growth for the business.

3. **How You Win.** This is your competitive strategy and articulates how you are advantaged against your competitors and what it is you are famous for. For example, Southwest airlines are famous for their low fares, McDonald's is famous for its ease and convenience, BMW is famous for product and engineering quality, Nordstroms is world famous for its service standards, and IBM is famous for delivering bespoke, customized solutions for its corporate clients. It's difficult, probably impossible, to be famous for all of these things at any one time, so, as with much of strategy, you have to choose. So, which of these points of fame—product leadership, cost leadership, convenience leadership, service leadership, or solutions leadership—are you pursuing? The answer is likely to be found where your customers' needs, your key capabilities, and your organizational passion meet.

4. **Your Agenda For Action.** These are the top three to six objectives you are implementing in order to deliver your #1 goal, establish your playing field, and enable you to win. In other words, it is the priorities you need to focus on to get you from where you are now to where you want to be. At Topps Tiles, for instance, the executive team has focused consistently on just three strategic objectives: range authority; delivering an inspirational shopping experience; and multichannel convenience. The specific projects within each of these objectives change from year-to-year but the objectives, like the company's #1 goal, remain. As with our second strategy management

principle, the management of Topps Tiles have remained fixed on the vision, but flexible on the journey.

So, in a dynamic and fast-changing world, the $100 million question is "How often should you change your strategy?" The answer is "Continuously," but the level of strategy change will depend on your own specific circumstances. Figure 4.2 shows a typical growth curve of a business, with early rapid growth that gradually turns into a plateau and ultimate decline, as mentioned in our third strategic principle that "nothing fails like success."

Using the growth curve in Figure 4.2, the ideal time to develop your next generation strategy and growth curve is at Position 1, but in most cases, management's desire to maximize the performance of the company's current success prevents any real development from taking place. Even at Position 2, when the level of success starts to plateau, management will aim to work harder at the current strategy and business model—for instance, launching extra product ranges and removing costs—in an attempt to raise performance and sustain success, rather than developing a

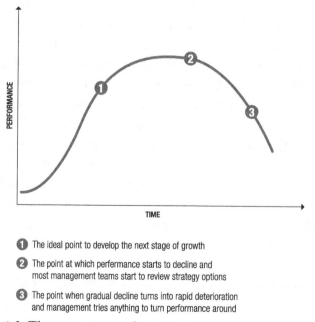

① The ideal point to develop the next stage of growth

② The point at which performance starts to decline and most management teams start to review strategy options

③ The point when gradual decline turns into rapid deterioration and management tries anything to turn performance around

Figure 4.2 The strategic growth curve

fundamentally different strategy. In fact, in most cases, it's only at Position 3, when the slow decline turns into more rapid performance collapse, that the ensuing crisis creates the impetus to develop something more radically different and new. Unfortunately, as we saw with Nokia, it is often too late at this point for any new strategy to have sufficient time to land effectively and deliver the desired level of growth, and the decline can quickly become terminal.

The level of change you need to attach to your strategy depends on your own performance and the ongoing and future level of change in your markets. I work on three different levels of strategic development with my clients, which I call the 3Rs of strategy:

- **Refinement.** All strategies need to be continuously refined if you are to hit your performance goals. For example, implementation projects will evolve to deliver better performance, the way you allocate resources will change to meet changes in your customers' needs and priorities, and you may need to make changes in the face of competitor moves. All of these things can take place without fundamentally altering any of the four elements of your "strategy arrow." For example, I recently worked with a U.K.-based manufacturing business that had set a clear goal for growth two years ago. Its most recent strategy review maintained its commitment to that goal, and our work focused on the best ways to accelerate the delivery of some of the existing key initiatives, rather than restarting the entire strategy process.
- **Renewal.** The second level of strategy development involves a more in-depth review of your chosen markets and a willingness to make major decisions to shift where you are investing for growth. Strategic renewal is not a complete transformation of your strategy, but it does involve making important changes to "where you play" or "how you win" to better fit your evolving markets and organization. For example, as I write, this morning's, *Financial Times* has reported that Procter & Gamble have decided to dispose of many of its major beauty brands, including Max Factor and

Wella, in order to focus investment on its higher-potential brands. Such a move is an example of renewal rather than refinement as it is clearly marking a shift in the scope of P&G's business.

- **Revolution.** Strategic revolution is the biggest level of change and involves fundamentally changing the direction of the business, requiring a distinctively different set of assets and capabilities. Apple's decision to move away from manufacturing Macs to becoming a major player in the global music and cell phone markets, for instance, is an example of strategic revolution, as is Intel's decision to focus on processors rather than memory and, here in the United Kingdom, the decision of Whitbread's executive to sell one of the country's oldest beer brewing businesses and, instead, focus on hotel, coffee, and leisure brands. As a consequence of the level of risk involved, revolutions are not common, but done well, they can propel your organization to its next generation of growth and success.

Going back to Figure 4.2, it may seem tempting to believe that you should focus on strategic refinement at Position 1 on the growth curve, renewal at Position 2, and revolution at Position 3. If that's what you do, however, you are more likely to experience the plateau and decline of the curve. Instead, you need to be working at all three levels continuously. At one high-performing client of mine, for instance, the CEO told me that he aimed to focus 80 percent of his time and effort on delivering the current year's performance (strategic refinement), 15 percent on ensuring success over the next two years (strategic renewal), and 5 percent on developing the capabilities necessary for success in the longer term (strategic revolution). The percentages may be different for your business, but the principle remains the same: you must work on all of the 3Rs in parallel if you are to avoid the perils of success and maximize your period of performance growth and success. The question we must answer now is how you can best manage that kind of strategy management process.

Organizing for Rapid-Fire Strategy

In the late 1990s, I took up my first major strategy role, leading the strategy team at the U.K. retail and pharmacy chain, Boots the Chemists. Back then, before the first Internet bubble had really been blown, the strategy process had a clear annual rhythm. Following my appointment, my diary quickly filled up with meetings and agendas that had been organized, in some cases, over a year in advance. Most strategy sessions were bunched into a couple of months of the year, at the start of the annual planning process. Over the rest of the year, we were expected to undertake strategy assessments and identify new growth opportunities, but many of our sessions with the Executive were tacked onto the end of operational meetings, rather than more focused strategic sessions.

Not long after I started my role, however, things changed for Boots—and not for the better! Wal-Mart's acquisition of the United Kingdom's third largest grocer, Asda, led to a price war with its key rivals, particularly Tesco. Health and Beauty, a relatively high-margin category for the grocers, was an effective battlefield for these retail giants, and Boots quickly began to suffer from collateral damage. Overnight, it seemed, the company's share price had fallen by a third as investors saw the value of the market evaporating and Boots' competitive position crumbling. As the price gap with the grocers widened, and the pressure on future growth and profit margins intensified, the sense of urgency—and periodic panic—took off like a rocket from the once-calm quarters of the executive corridor.

While we had previously talked about the need for greater pace and stronger differentiation, as well as the rising intensity of competition, our actions and our diaries reflected a belief that we were still in control of events. Not any longer—we needed a different approach. In the space of three months, I had led a cross-functional team of senior managers on a full-time project to develop radically alternative business models, run a series of strategy "away days" for the executive team, and undertaken reviews of pricing, cost, and growth strategies. Some of the ideas and initiatives that resulted from this work helped to improve the company's competitive position and performance; others didn't. The interesting point, however, was that the reaction to greater chaos, uncertainty, and turbulence was more strategy, not less.

So, how do you organize for effective strategy management in the 21st century? I suggest an approach that incorporates five specific elements:

1. **Annual Strategy Summit.** I believe that there is still room for an in-depth, no-holds-barred annual strategy review for most businesses. In terms of the 3Rs of strategy, these sessions need to be focused on "Renewal" and "Revolution," incorporating a fundamental review of your business, its markets, and leading to the development and review of distinctive options for future growth. You may end up with a refinement of your existing strategy, but you will have done so having critically assessed real alternatives, giving you more confidence in your underlying approach.

   For the past five years, for instance, I have run an annual strategy summit process for the executive team of a homewares business that has sought to test its existing strategy against a range of mutually exclusive alternatives. The process has allowed the team to kick the tires of its strategy and each year has enabled the team to shift resources into new priorities. There have been no huge single strategic "revolutions," but five years on, the strategy is very different from its original focus. For instance, the company has now significantly grown its trade business, has opened new digital sales and distribution channels, developed a highly successful loyalty program, and become an avatar for customer service in its industry. Each of these new priorities emerged from the executive team's annual strategy summit and the team's willingness to openly challenge its existing direction and refocus the company's priorities.

2. **Half-Yearly Growth Summit.** If the annual strategy summit is a forum for the executive team, and selected senior managers, to thrash out major strategic alternatives, a six-monthly growth summit enables a far broader set of managers to become involved in identifying and developing potential new growth opportunities and engaging with the leadership team on their relative merits. In Chapter 5, Fast-Lane Innovation, we'll discuss how you can involve your teams in creating a faster, more effective innovation process for your business, but the growth summit acts as an effective starting point for radical growth.

   The aim of the summit is to identify a handful of new growth ideas—probably no more than two or three—that you agree to develop in the following few weeks and months. In addition to the executive team, managers from across the business are invited to the summit, along with external experts who can add further value to the discussions. For example, I recently worked with around 25 senior managers from a $500-million U.K. retailer on a one-and-half-day growth summit. The end point of our discussions was a decision to pursue three new major growth priorities: to enter a major new geographical region; to investigate four specific new acquisitions; and to test and trial a radical new approach to home delivery. During the course of the summit, over 30 separate ideas were discussed and considered, but these were whittled down to these three priorities. Critically, the list was agreed by the entire group, not simply the CEO or executive team, further building commitment to their delivery. In the following week, further kick-off meetings were held for each of these priorities, leaders appointed, and project milestones established to accelerate their delivery.

3. **Quarterly Priority Reviews.** When a new leader joins a business, they often create a 90-day or 100-day plan. I think that this period is great for focusing effort—three months is enough time to get some serious work done, but short enough to keep the pressure on delivery. What I don't understand is why more executives don't have ongoing 90-day plans rather than an initial, one-off exercise?

   Given the turbulence and dynamic nature of many markets, three months is also a good period for managing organizational priorities and activities. Some programs and initiatives can take years to deliver, but most can be broken down into quarterly milestones and, if you focus effectively, you can make rapid progress on some of your most important issues within a three-month time frame. At one retail client, for example, a new CEO decided to focus on the single metric of product availability for the first three months of his tenure. Availability had been a perennial problem at the retailer, despite major investments in systems, but the new CEO's focus on this single issue created the energy and collective focus required to improve availability levels by 10 percent and grow sales by 2 percent in that initial quarter.

4. **Monthly Strategy Sessions.** I have mentioned above that an annual strategy summit can create the ability to undertake a fundamental review of your business. But this is best achieved if you have more regular strategy sessions with your team. This approach enables you

to build up the shared knowledge and insights of your business, your markets, your customers, and your competitors that create the confidence for the bigger decisions that can come out of the annual reviews. As surveys have shown, big strategic decisions rarely come out of the big setpiece, annual reviews, but from the more regular meetings, and the corridor conversations that surround them. As Peter Birtles, the CEO of the Super Retail Group in Australia once told me, "As the leadership team has developed I have found it is the more regular, less formal meetings and conversations where our key strategic objectives and initiatives are really developed."

5. **Weekly Big Idea Reviews.** As we shall see in Chapter 5, effective innovation is both a strategic imperative and a messy process of development, testing, and refinement. If this process is to work, you need to have regular updates and reviews. One way of doing this that cuts the chain of command between the ideas and the leadership team is to have weekly "big idea" reviews. In these sessions, new, big ideas are presented worked on, reviewed, and updated. During the turnaround of U.K. grocer, Asda, in the early 1990s, the executive team met each Monday morning at a local store that had been set up as a laboratory to run a series of experiments and to test new ideas. The team walked the store, reviewed the week's progress, and agreed the priorities for the following seven days. The pace of innovation at Asda rapidly accelerated, and its subsequent growth and profitability attracted Wal-Mart sufficiently to buy the business.

The 6-Day Strategy: Why Spend 6 Months Developing a 1-Year Plan?

The five strategy forums described above provide an ongoing way to manage strategy and to ensure that your overall direction, strategic priorities, and key initiatives remain relevant, focused, and successful in fast-changing markets. But there is one more issue that we need to address: strategy development simply takes too long. In a world where plans rarely last a year, it makes little sense to spend six months or more on the development of those plans. A new mind-set and new approaches are needed to create a robust and compelling strategy at pace. *The 6-Day Strategy* is a tool that can help you set the direction, and generate the focus necessary for you to succeed at a pace that is 20 times faster than traditional approaches.

An overview of *The 6-Day Strategy* is shown in Figure 4.3. The process provides a logical and natural flow for the discussion and dialogue

DAY	OBJECTIVE	KEY QUESTIONS	INPUTS
1 Our current position	Define the key issues and opportunities facing the business over the next 1-3 years	• What do customers think of us? • How effective is our financial performance? • How attractive are our markets? • How strong are our competitive positions?	• Customer research • Financial reviews • Market assessments • Strategic position assessments • Competitor reviews
2 Future possibilities	Identify growth options beyond the next 3 years	• How could our markets evolve? • What new opportunities might be created? • What are the capabilities for future success? • What are the implications for us?	• Market forecasts • Reviews of other, similar markets • Reviews of new, high-growth competitors and 'leading edge' customers • Social and technology trends
3 Setting the direction	Agree our core strategic direction	• What are our top goals? What's our #1 goal? • How should our 'playing field' evolve? • How will we win? What are the competitive advantages we need to secure and develop?	• Outputs from the first two days
4 Defining the organisation	Determine the priorities for executive focus	• What are the critical organizational capabilities we need to develop? • What kind of talent do we need – now and in the future? • How should we best engage and involve our people? • How will we lead this organization?	• Output from Day 3 • Talent assessments • Organizational engagement scores • Operational scorecards • Future capabilities assessments
5 Shaping the agenda	Determine the priorities for executive focus	• What do we need to focus on to deliver our emerging strategy? • What are our executive priorities? • What are the underlying goals, objectives and milestones? • Who will be accountable for delivery?	• Outputs from Day 3 and Day 4 • Talent assessments • Existing performance objectives
6 Preparing for launch	Establish how you will lead and manage the execution of the strategy	• How will we communicate, involve and engage our people in the next stage of work? • How will we manage the key programs of activity? • What are the key risks of this strategy and how will we manage them? • Are we fully aligned on our new strategy and next steps?	• Outputs from Day 3, 4 and 5 • Program management best practices • Communication and engagement best practices

Figure 4.3 The 6-day strategy

necessary to develop a clear and compelling strategy for your company. Many executive teams, in addition to using consultants to create strategy proposals for the business, also run annual strategy off-sites, for a day or two, or put half a day or more in the diary every few months. In my experience, however, these sessions can lack focus. Urgent operational matters are added to the agenda, for instance, to make best use of the executive team's time together, and discussions can simply end up focusing on the previous few weeks' or months' trading, rather than developing a deeper and more fundamental understanding of your strategic direction.

A structured and disciplined approach is needed to ensure that you make rapid and relevant progress. Perhaps surprisingly, a robust structure also enables you to be more creative in your thinking, and a well-designed strategy process that involves your key players effectively, can have a transformative effect on the future success of your business. The process can act as a springboard for new and better ways to implement the strategy.

There are five fundamental elements of *The 6-Day Strategy* that help ensure success:

1. Executive Involvement and Leadership

The development of your organization's future strategy should never be delegated to an external consultant, or summarized onto a presentation for sign-off. Delivering a new growth strategy is hard work, and executives must fully own the goals they are setting for their business. This can only be achieved through direct involvement, not through detached assessment.

As Dennis Sadlowski, the former CEO of Siemens Energy in the United States, once said to me about the approach he took to strategy development with his management teams, "Engagement starts with involvement, and I ensured that the executive team and key managers at the next level were intimately involved in the development of our growth strategy. We didn't rely on external consultants to tell us the way forward; we led the work ourselves, doing our own blocking and tackling to make sure we understood the detail."

This means that, as leaders of your business, you must be willing to dedicate the time together, engage with the critical issues and opportunities facing your organization, and work through the alternatives to find the best strategy. Setting the future direction of the business and establishing the critical priorities are two of the biggest roles of any leadership team. Managing operational performance can be delegated to other managers; setting strategy cannot. As with Dennis Sadlowski, this doesn't mean you can't invite other key mangers to get involved—although the process becomes slower and more cumbersome if you have more than, say, 10 or so people in the room—but the entire executive team should be fully involved in the entire process to maximize the results.

2. Future Focus

Just because this is a rapid strategy process does not mean that it should just deal with the short-term issues of the business or create a series of "quick wins." Six days is ample time to review what's happening at the leading edges of your markets and to peer over the horizon at new opportunities and emerging realities and trends. Think big, use this opportunity to have team discussions that you perhaps haven't had before, and you may just find that you unearth previously hidden growth ideas and concepts.

Day 2 is specifically focused on thinking beyond the immediate future of the business. Given the turbulence and dynamic nature of most markets, it is critical that you don't simply project current trends, but that you also look for potential discontinuities and shifts in your business. Taking the effort to consider what your customers will be doing in more than a couple of years' time can also help you consider more fundamental and step change improvements to your proposition and your organization.

As a result, you may want to bring in specialists from outside your industry, or experts in technology, social trends, or innovation into the session to help stimulate new thinking. Alternatively, you may want to design and go through more creative exercises.

As part of one of our strategy projects, for example, a retail leadership team worked to create three alternative futures for their industry and, on the basis of the insights gained, identified five new growth ideas they hadn't previously identified. Alternatively, a consumer goods client stepped into the future by asking what would happen to their business if

Google acquired it. Again, this process of breaking away from the current business and market realities led to new growth ideas for the leadership team to consider.

3.   Preparation and Support

The quality of the results of the strategy process is directly dependent on two factors: (1) the quality of the preparation and inputs and (2) the quality of the discussions and dialogue of the team. We'll deal with the second success factor in point 4, below, but in terms of the preparation and inputs, there are three critical areas you need to focus on:

1. **A Robust Factbase.** In too many strategy sessions, there is simply too much data. People end up getting lost in the analysis and lose sight of the key issues at stake. With data, it's not the quantity that counts; it's the quality that's paramount. Facts are needed so that conversations aren't merely the sharing of different opinions and that a mirror is held up to the leadership team to make sure they focus on the realities of their situation, but the focus of the discussions need to be on the future and how you will address your agreed issues and opportunities. A 10-to-20-page insight pack covering financial, customer, competitive, and market insights will provide a suitable point of reference for the meetings without confusing everyone by providing information overload.

2. **Participant Preparation.** Everyone should come to the initial meeting with a clear understanding of the objectives, their role and initial views, ideas, and questions. This requires a structured approach to briefing that should include the following:
   - An introductory conversation with the owner of the process (usually the CEO or equivalent) and the key facilitator (see point 4, below) to provide an overview of the process and to gain initial feedback and respond to any questions.
   - A focused questionnaire, designed and collated by the facilitator, on key questions and hot topics, to gauge the initial thoughts of the participants and to help stimulate thinking and to finesse the design of the process.

- Sharing the factbase a week or so ahead of the strategy process, together with one or two relevant articles—possibly concerning the future of your industry, interesting new management thinking, or new approaches to one or more of your critical processes (such as innovation). As with the factbase, though, the key is not to overload the participants with data, but to provide sufficient initial food for thought to fuel the initial conversations.

- An initial mini-project for each of the participants. In addition to the questionnaire and factbase, we have found that giving participants a small, say two-hour, assignment ahead of the initial session also helps to get the juices flowing. This can be done in pairs or small groups, rather than individually. At one company, for example, pairs of participants reviewed selected companies in completely different industries and were tasked with identifying three new ideas for growth that they believed could be transferred into their business.

3. **Support Team.** Throughout the six days, you will raise plenty of questions. Not all of these can be answered immediately, but you will find that many of them can be resolved with a little background analysis and research. We've found that having a small support team—covering finance, marketing, operations, and HR—can help to sort out these issues as the meetings progress, helping to build and maintain the momentum of the sessions.

4. *Structure and Facilitation*

In Figure 4.3, we've set out an overview of the areas of discussion for each day of the *The 6-Day Strategy* process. In reality, however, no two processes are the same. Each organization is unique and while the overall flow will be similar between different businesses, the specific design of the meetings will be different. Each day needs to be designed according to the company's needs and the ongoing outcomes of the sessions.

This means that a dedicated meeting designer should be involved to ensure that the specific topics, the tools and frameworks used, and the specific activities that enable the team to reach clear, robust, and aligned conclusions in the fastest time possible. A clear structure also requires, in most cases, that an independent facilitator is used to guide and moderate the discussion, enabling the CEO or meeting leader to focus on the content of the meeting rather than being overly concerned with managing the process.

5. Maintaining the Momentum

Each day of *The 6-Day Strategy* has a different objective and questions to answer, as shown in Figure 4.3. This ensures that you build up momentum and make rapid progress and development. Over the six days, you might not answer all the questions you identify as a team, but don't let a search for perfection drive out success. After all, it's far easier to change direction once you're moving, than it is to try and turn the wheel when you're at a standstill.

It's also possible, of course, to breakdown the six days into a series of shorter sessions. This works equally well if you maintain the focus over a two- or three-week period, but if you end up spreading out the sessions over two or three months, you're hardly any further forward from more traditional strategy approaches. What's more, you also end up taking time to reconnect with the work to date, and team members can become detached from the outputs of the work.

Making it Happen

Developing a new strategy for your business is only the start of a process of change and improvement. As you launch the outputs of your work, you must continue to involve, engage, and align your people around your new goals and priorities. What's more, the strategy will inevitably evolve in the face of new environmental realities and your own experience of implementation: some things will work, others won't. *The 6-Day Strategy* kick-starts this positive cycle of success, helping to make sure that your organization doesn't simply spin its strategic wheels, but gets into gear and starts to make things happen at a pace that is at least in line with rate of change in your markets.

As you and your colleagues become aligned around your future direction, other positive changes will emerge. Managers will find it easier to make decisions, for instance. They will also see that the leaders of their organization have acted quickly and decisively to move the business forward. Once sustained, these positive behaviors translate into a company that is not only faster, but one that is also more confident, more responsive, and far more proactive. In other words, *The 6-Day Strategy* can help your organization develop the traits of companies that win, and win fast.

CHAPTER 5

Fast-Lane Innovation

Releasing the Innovation Brakes

There was a time, not that long ago, when companies didn't necessarily have an innovation-related objective on their strategic agenda. Instead, they would, for example, be focused on reducing costs, expanding geographically or creating operational excellence. It wasn't that product or service development wasn't important, it was just that the level of detailed executive and organizational focus on this area of the business varied in line with its perceived relevance to the company's growth ambitions.

As Bob Dylan once sang, though, *things have changed*. Innovation is no longer a strategic alternative; it is a strategic imperative. It is impossible to gain and sustain a leading position in your market without a systematic and comprehensive commitment to innovation. As we have seen in the first four chapters, the pace of change in all markets means that you must be constantly adapting and changing at least as fast as your environment. And if, as we discussed in Chapter 4, *nothing fails like success*, it's incumbent on you to continuously raise the bar on your performance and find new ways to win, rather than simply relying on your perpetuating your existing successes.

Innovation is, of course, far more than product and service development. In corporate terms, innovation can be seen as the delivery of an important and original idea that provides you with new competitive advantages. When you take this wider view of innovation, you can quickly identify different types:

- **Product and Service Innovation.** This is what most people mean when they talk about innovation. Dyson's bagless vacuum cleaner, Apple's iPad, and Nespresso coffee capsules are all examples of product innovations that have fundamentally shifted the dynamics of their market. More than that, these products have expertly met customers' latent and unmet needs and have created new market segments, enabling these products to deliver superior levels of growth and profitability. Even with patent, trademark and brand protection, however, the competitive advantages offered by these products are eroded over time through competition. Even with game-changing innovations, entropy will inevitably take over and your advantages, revenues, and cash flows will decline. Relying on single-hit innovations, rather than a stream—or even a torrent—of new innovations, will not create sustainable success.

- **Operational Innovation.** Some companies drive innovations through their operating model, often led by investment in technology. During the 1980s and 1990s, for example, Wal-Mart gained huge advantages against Kmart and its other rivals through the company's massive and sophisticated investment in supply chain systems and technologies. Unlike product innovation, however, you are far less likely to be able to protect such innovations with patents and trademarks, unless you were willing to make the investment in proprietary technologies, and so any competitive advantage you accrue are at even greater risk of decay. Again, as your rivals catch up, you will be required to find the next stage innovation if you wish to maintain or extend your operational advantage.

- **Business Model Innovation.** It's possible to innovate at an even higher level than product or operations. In Europe, Ryanair and other low-fare airlines, for instance, have transformed the air travel market by creating and deploying an entirely new business model that traditional carriers find difficult to compete against. The limited service, use of less popular and costly airports, rapid turnarounds, and use of a single type of aircraft (the Boeing 737 being most common) enables these companies to run at costs far below the bigger, full-service airlines that are focused on their hub and spoke business models. Product innovation can also go hand in hand with business model innovation. Nespresso, for instance, not only sells a range of coffee capsules, but also does so through a system that the company either controls or strongly influences. The coffee machines can only use Nespresso capsules and the capsules can only be bought through company's online portal or from its small chain of boutique stores; they are not available in grocers or other retailers. Innovations focused around entire business models are harder to copy than product or operational innovations, but are equally harder to develop and deliver.

- **Organizational and Cultural Innovation.** Finally, companies can innovate around their culture and organization. In the 1980s, for example, ABB created a high-growth business by breaking the huge engineering company into a series of smaller and entrepreneurial business units. Back in the 1930s, Alfred Sloan created a scientific, profit-focused, and strategic approach to management at General Motors, which shaped how generations of managers approached their own businesses. More recently, Toyota has developed a brand and business success on the back of a cultural approach to quality management at the auto manufacturer that puts the focus on the line teams to manage their own performance. And in 2009, Amazon paid $1.2 billion for a shoe retailer that only started trading in 2000. The rise of Zappos was driven by the relentless focus of its leadership team on customer service, and the development of an organizational culture that provides a great experience for its workers, encouraging them to go the extra mile for their customers. In other words, it is possible to create a serious competitive advantage through your organization, management approach, and culture that other companies can find hard to match.

INNOVATION
DELIVERED

LOST
OPPORTUNITY

INNOVATION
POTENTIAL

Figure 5.1 The innovation gap

Using this broader view, you can immediately see that the potential for better and faster innovation in many businesses is huge. In most organizations, however, there is a yawning gulf between senior leaders' rhetoric on innovation and the reality on the ground, which I call "the innovation gap" (see Figure 5.1).

The creativity, invention, and commercial acumen that is required for fast-lane innovation exists in most organizations. It is just that in some businesses it is better hidden than in others. Like a gardener preparing the beds for the best blooms, your job as a leader of your business is to nurture, protect, and feed your people's willingness and ability to identify and deliver a stream of innovation. And, as any gardener will tell you, to make that happen you must first get rid of the weeds.

The "lost opportunity" set out in the chart is not generally a result of poor intentions, but is a consequence of specific barriers that lurk unseen in many businesses. I call these barriers the "innovation brakes," and they fall into three types:

1. **Strategic Brakes.** The decisions you take to set the future ambition and direction of your business, and the way in which you manage its delivery, directly impacts on your ability to innovate. Incremental goals, an unwillingness to cannibalize sales before your competitors cannibalize them for you, and simply pursuing too many priorities can slow down and stop your level and pace of innovation.

2. **Organizational Brakes.** Even if you create a strategy that systematically drives innovation, you will still see limited progress unless you address the organizational brakes on the pace and scale of innovation. These brakes include a reliance on a small internal cadre of innovators, unclear accountabilities, and an excessive planning focus. Creating an organization that can innovate at pace means actively addressing and removing these brakes from your business.

3. **Cultural Brakes.** Finally, the pace and scale of innovation is also driven by the culture and attitudes that prevail in your organization. Your attitude to risk, and your approach to business growth, is highlighted, for instance, by whether you look for a one-off "magic pill" solution to your sales growth issues or seek to create a "daily exercise regime" for innovation. Similarly, companies pursuing a fast-lane innovation strategy will be willing to lead and not just follow their customers' stated needs and will ensure that senior managers are able to accept and even innovation failures, particularly where that failure was achieved quickly and cheaply and was the result of a manager's willingness to take prudent risks to lead, rather than follow your markets.

Achieving your "innovation potential" requires you to identify and release these brakes. As you do so, you will see that both the scale and speed of innovation delivered by your organization will accelerate. And, as with personal success and development, changing your attitudes and beliefs will have the biggest and most sustainable impact on your company's performance. This means that innovation must be led from the top. It is the chief executive, or equivalent, who sets the tone for the rest of the business, and the innovation tune the CEO plays must be sufficiently clear, consistent, and catchy for the rest of the business to join in.

Building Up Speed: Focusing Innovation on What Won't Change

Amazon has led a transformation of the retail sector. From a standing start at the turn of the century, it is currently the most important retailer on the planet, even though it doesn't own a single physical store. By any definition you care to use, Amazon is an innovative business. But there is a secret to Amazon's ability to innovate and grow faster than its rivals.

Amazon's approach to innovation has been different. Rather than primarily focusing on the constant changes in the desires and needs of its various customer segments, the company has pinned its innovation activities on what won't change. For Amazon, the company has centered on three customer needs that Bezos and his leadership team have identified: range, price, and delivery speed. They took the decision that these factors will remain important to their customers over years and decades, not simply months and quarters. In many ways, these areas of focus look simple, even a little boring. But they have been critical to the company's success (see Figure 5.2).

The company's ability to focus on these factors has led to three key benefits:

1. **Bigger, Bolder, and More Disruptive Initiatives.** While its more traditional rivals have hedged their bets with investments across various channels, Amazon has been able to single-mindedly invest in its online business. The company's incessant focus on the needs and wants of its customers has also led it to make some big, bold decisions that have not only disrupted the market, but also the existing Amazon business model. Take the *Marketplace* concept, for instance. Most retailers look to control price and margins by buying and offering their products themselves, with no internal competition. The *Marketplace* has turned that thinking on its head. Amazon's own product buyers now face competition on Amazon's own real estate from third-party sellers who can offer both new and used versions of the product, and who can also offer ranges to shoppers that are not offered by Amazon.

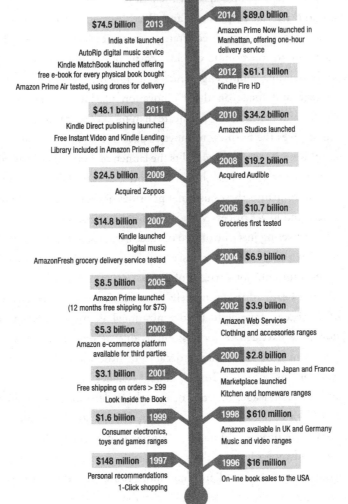

Figure 5.2 Amazon's innovation landmarks

The downside of this decision is the risk that it lowers Amazon's revenues and profits. It is also likely to create more than a little angst across the buying teams! The upside is that the *Marketplace* elegantly meets Amazon's stated commitment to focus on customers' need for greater choice and lower prices. The concept may create some tactical difficulties for Amazon, but, strategically, it hits the bull's eye, particularly as it gives eBay competition for small independent retailers looking for a wide, national or global market. And if the decision has affected revenues and returns, it is hard to spot any downside within Amazon's reported results over the past few years.

2. **Organizational Alignment and Pace.** Amazon's consistent innovation focus on just three strategic priorities has also enabled the company to move more quickly. Focus builds understanding, and understanding builds engagement, alignment, and pace. Amazon's strategy and focus on three innovation platforms is far simpler, clearer, and easier to communicate than most corporation's strategies and enables the business to move at pace in a style that is similar to Southwest. Figure 5.2 highlights the launch of Amazon's major innovations between its launch in 1996 and 2014 and how they impact on the company's three customer priorities of greater choice, delivery speed, and lower prices. Most successful businesses would be happy with delivering just one or two of these game-changing innovations, but Amazon's focus and consistency have enabled the company to create a torrent, not a stream of innovation into its markets.

3. **Market Leadership.** Ultimately, Amazon's interconnected elements of consistent strategic focus, organizational alignment, and innovation pace have led to its position as one of retail's global market leaders in little more than a decade. In little more than 10 years, Amazon has become a Top 20 Global Retailer in terms of revenues and the retail leader in terms of thought leadership. If the company had followed most of its rivals' approaches, its strategy would have been more diverse and more responsive to changes in the competitive landscape of its markets. As a result, its portfolio of projects would have been less aligned and more cluttered and the company's managers would have been less clear about what was truly important. In turn, this would have created a sluggish, slow, and incremental business that followed, rather than led its markets. Strategic success happens when you are the first to profit from opportunities that are created by the dynamics of technological, social, and economic developments. Amazon's multichannel, traditional rivals have struggled to keep up because they do not have the purity of

Amazon's strategic focus. Their lack of true strategic and innovation commitment reduces the pace of these organizations and diminishes their ability to become a market leader.

Shifting Gear: Acceleration Through Action

Convenience has always been important to grocery shoppers. For most of us, the weekly grocery shop is not a source of pleasure and delight, but is a chore that must be done—as quickly and as easily as possible. Back in the 1990s—or, as I tell my children, in the dim and distant days before the iPhone was a twinkle in Steve Jobs' eye—two U.K. grocery giants were battling for supremacy. The traditional market leader, Sainsbury's, was being overtaken by Tesco, a focused and aggressive business that had a clear customer strategy of ease and convenience for the United Kingdom's time-starved shoppers, under the tagline of "Every Little Helps." Both retailers had been working on reducing customer queuing time at the checkout. Customer research will tell you that queuing to pay ranks just above having your fingernails removed with pliers in shoppers' list of dislikes, so finding a cost-effective solution to this issue was a big opportunity for both rivals.

Tesco's team had been struggling to make the financials work for its new service model, and was still refining its approach when management received word that Sainsbury's were ready to go live with their solution. Management had a decision to make. Should they let Sainsbury's be first to market with a better and faster queuing system, in the hope that once they had refined their own model customers would see that it was superior, or should they just launch their approach immediately and be seen as the queuing and convenience innovator in the market? The team decided to press the button and launch their solution ahead of Sainsbury's. Tesco's "One In Front" policy, where the retailer promised to open up the next available till if there was more than one person in the queue ahead of you, was an immediate success. Even though Sainsbury's launched its own solution a matter of days later, all the kudos and brand benefit was bestowed on Tesco. If Sainsbury's policy had a name, I have no idea what it was. Their solution was irrelevant as Tesco's flag was already firmly placed on that queue-busting summit. By being first to market—even with a solution that was not perhaps fully market-ready—Tesco was able to further tighten its grip on the U.K. grocery market. Being first had trumped being best.

In some markets—commercial jet engines, for example—every factor should be fully tested in all conditions before going into production. I would certainly prefer, for instance, that all the side effects of any prescribed drug I was asked to take had been fully understood and addressed before they were dispatched to my local pharmacy. But most of you aren't in the jet engine, pharmaceutical, or other life-threatening industries. Rapid, timely action, rather than further planning, is the key to success for most innovations. Here are five steps you can take to move your innovation into your market's fast lane:

1. **Clarify the Concept.** All innovation starts with an idea. The critical task at the idea stage is to be clear about the concept, and how the new product, service, or organizational approach will both work and improve performance. Often, a simple chart or visual helps to develop the required clarity. Southwest Airlines founder, Herb Kelleher, for instance, famously drew a triangle on a cocktail bar napkin to demonstrate how a new airline serving Houston, Dallas, and San Antonio in Texas could operate.

2. **Build a Series of Rapid Prototypes.** Version #1 is rarely completely successful. Neither are versions #2, 3, 4, or 10. You will fail with your initial prototypes. The idea is not to avoid failure, but to learn, adapt, and improve as quickly and as cheaply as you can. A critical element is to make sure that you don't "gold plate" your prototype; just make it good enough to allow you to learn quickly. We're not talking about months and months here, we're talking about days and weeks. Have a go, see what works, fix what doesn't and try again.

3. **Get Early, Objective Feedback.** Toward the end of the idea generation workshops that I lead, I ask the team to present their emerging ideas to a panel of real customers. This stage in the process has two big advantages. First, it ensures that the team involved in the workshop develops real ideas that they can articulate and explain to "normal" people. There is no room for buzzwords or theoretical concepts; the ideas must be clear and practical. Second, the customers can

provide immediate feedback on the ideas, enabling the development teams to more clearly focus on the next stage of their work. I believe that early customer feedback is vital to the innovation process, but don't expect to receive 100 percent approval. The more innovative your concept, the more likely it is that there will be resistance and distrust of it as people take time to come round to more radical ideas. Your aim is to gain evidence that your target customers believe that the idea has the potential to deliver genuine customer benefits.

4. **Confirm the Business Model Potential.** This is the step that might take time, but which is crucial to longer-term success. It marks the difference between pace and haste. Google founders Larry Page and Sergey Brin, for instance, spent two years or more searching for a profitable business model for their search engine before they settled on an advertising-driven model that enabled them to fully expand the service and drive its subsequent relentless growth. Two years may seem a long time, but sometimes you need to balance pace with patience. Brin and Page could have gone with their first business model concept, but that may have led to the company's early demise. Instead, they waited until they had an "80 percent solution," which has been fundamental to the company's amazing success.

5. **Launch Phase 1—*and* Develop Phases 2, 3, and 4.** The launch of an innovation is not the end of the process; it is the beginning. You should see the delivery of a new innovation to your organization or your market as an ongoing process not a one-off event. Even before Version 1 of your innovation is in use, your teams should be developing the next one or two versions so that you build up both pace and momentum. Apple's management of the iPod product development process has been a great example of this approach. In just a few years from its initial launch, Apple delivered a series of updates to the iPod range that offered both greater storage capacity and functionality at lower prices. The iPod didn't succeed so spectacularly because of the initial version, but because of the stream of constantly improving, market leading, and increasingly value-for-money products that customers absolutely loved. The combination of bigger storage capacity, improved functionality, better design and lower prices, and the pace at which Apple managed its product innovation pipeline also

made it exceptionally difficult for potential rivals such as Sony or Microsoft to mount an effective competitive strategy, enabling Apple to dominate this niche until and beyond the launch of the iPhone.

These five steps rely on higher levels of management judgment, commitment and prudent risk-taking than more conservative, risk-averse, and planning-led innovation approaches. That said, I am not advocating a kamikaze approach where you simply close your eyes and hope for the best, but neither am I suggesting that you should have total confidence in your solution before moving. If you are to accelerate innovation through action, you must be open to new ideas and approaches, to trust your judgment, to seek out and learn from objective, customer-centered feedback, and to give your teams the confidence to commit to implementation, showing them that they can refine and improve any problems along the way.

8 Accelerators for Fast-Lane Innovation

So what practical organizational tools can you put in place to give you and your teams the confidence to adopt an action-led approach that can deliver fast-lane innovation? Here are eight innovation accelerators that you can pursue.

Accelerator #1: Establish a Clear Innovation Ambition

The level and pace of innovation within a business is, to a large extent, driven by its culture and the attitude and behaviors of its most senior leaders. Yet, even in a slower, more conservative organization, there are ways to rapidly and dramatically step change the level and speed at which you introduce new products, services, operational improvements, and management approaches. The first step is to establish and communicate a clear ambition, or set of ambitions, for innovation.

A common goal is to set a certain percentage of sales from products and services launched in the past, say, three years. This is fine as far as it goes, but I have seen examples of such goals where the percentage is set so low, and where the time frame is five years or more, that there is no real stimulus to innovate. There are other goals and ambitions you can set that will create greater levels of change in your business. For instance,

- Establish a $ sales and profit goal for products and services launched in the last one, two, and three years. People understand $ far more easily than they understand percentage, and as it's easier to keep score, it's also easier for your organization to engage around your ambition. Creating short-term, as well as long-term goals, also helps create and maintain the pressure for change and action.
- Compare your level of innovation to your key rivals, and set a goal so that you have, say, 50 percent more of your sales and profits from new products and services than any other player in your market. Using this goal ensures that you're not only improving over time, but also that your competitive position is getting stronger.
- Set a target to become the #1 for innovation for your target customers. Once your customers view you as innovative, your corporate brand and reputation will be enhanced, enabling you, over time, to add a premium to prices and gain a larger share of your markets. If you're improving performance, but are still in the pack, you won't gain this recognition, but if your underlying ambition is to be seen as the innovation leader, you will find that your people will start to make different decisions and take different actions in pursuit of that higher-level goal.

How clear is your organization's innovation ambition, and what steps can you take to make it sharper, clearer, and easier to deliver?

Accelerator #2: Ensure the Same Person Runs the R&D and Sales Teams

The teams responsible for R&D and product and service innovation commonly report into a Chief Marketing Officer or Chief Technology Officer. Innovation, it seems, is seen as too important to be placed under the responsibility of operators. And yet, in entrepreneurial start-up companies, which tend to be more innovative than the bigger corporations they aspire to become, the owner/chief executive drives innovation directly. This person is also responsible for sales, and it is this direct link that generates the pace of development and success.

I have seen companies where the sales teams will not accept many new products being developed and brought to market, do not trust that their customers will appreciate them, and give them little more than lip service. At one client of mine, for example, less than 50 percent of the country markets had deployed the last three major product launches because they didn't believe they were relevant to their customers.

A simple, straightforward organizational solution to this issue is to bring innovation, research and development, and sales under a single team. After all, it is the sales teams that are closest to your customers and have the best understanding of their needs. Bringing innovation and sales under the same leadership provides a direct linkage between customer opportunities and new product and service possibilities. It is exactly how the best, most entrepreneurial business operate and it could enable you to step change the pace, and take-up of new products and services by both your sales teams and your customers.

How closely are your innovation and sales teams aligned, and what steps can you take to bring the two teams under a single point of control?

Accelerator #3: Recruit People With a Bias for Innovation

There is a difference between good managers and innovation leaders. As companies grow and mature, they attract and retain a bigger number of "good managers." These people are effective at implementing projects, resolving issues, planning, performance management, communicating with their teams, and delivering ongoing, incremental improvements. They do not, in general, however, possess the appetite for risk, the desire to experiment, and the willingness to fail that sets "innovation leaders" apart.

If you want greater levels of innovation, the answer is simple: recruit more "innovation leaders." The issue is that these people do not always have the best qualifications or a track record of seamless success and a faultless rise through the ranks. They are likely to have failures as well as successes on their CV, to have taken sideways or downward career path decisions, and may not always have some of the basic skills demonstrated by "good managers." Nevertheless, without more "innovation leaders" in your team, you will never step, change the level of innovation in your business.

How many innovation leaders are there in your company, and what steps could you take to increase their numbers and influence?

Accelerator #4: Embed a Simple, Organization-wide Innovation Process

Far from inhibiting the scale and pace of innovation, a simple process, understood by all can accelerate progress. Critically, the process should be focused on speed not bureaucracy. Increasing the number and pace of ideas in your business should not be about form-filling, but about capturing the energy, imagination, and commercial creativity of your people. Key elements include the following:

- *The CEO Must Lead the Process.* Symbolically, this emphasizes the importance of innovation to the company, and it also encourages others to get involved. What's more, many organizational structures inhibit innovation: different departments have different objectives and priorities, inhibiting people's ability to work together. Top-level leadership helps you cut-through and overcome these barriers.
- *Create Standard Approaches.* You need standard approaches so that managers and teams from different parts of the business can communicate and work together. Establish common ways of generating ideas, managing funding, and reviewing performance.
- *Train Managers on the Process.* Your people must have the skills before they can contribute to your innovation process. As they apply these skills, the results will improve, but a starting point in idea generation, understanding possible prizes, project management, and seeking and securing funding are all areas where some initial education will pay off.

- *Focus on Rapid Testing.* Many large organizations agonize on a best approach. It's far better, however, to try something out. Having a central kitty to fund simple, early prototypes (no more than a few $ thousands at any one time) allows you to test your ideas quickly with customers, and will give you a better understanding of what will work than a pile of academic customer research.
- *Back the Winners.* Rapid testing will give you a feel for what will work and what won't. This enables you to then focus on and back the winners. At this point, you can create a balance between those ideas that are likely to give a rapid payback (say, less than 12 months) and those which will require a longer-term investment.

How simple is your innovation process, and how well do your people know how to get involved in it?

Accelerator #5: Allow Time Each Week for Innovation Projects—for Everyone

Many innovations are created by small teams (two or three people) working together on small ideas, rather than by individuals working independently or as part of larger, more formal collaborations. What can you do to encourage these "skunk works" in your business? Some companies, including Google and 3M, let their people spend a proportion of their working week on projects that are of interest to a small group, rather than as part of a wider corporate initiative. There are four elements to help you make this approach succeed:

- *Build and Raise Capabilities.* You must invest in the skills and capabilities required for effective innovation. These include creative thinking approaches, prototype development, team leadership and project management, as well as relevant technical and engineering skills. Not only should you invest in the development of your existing teams, but you should also ensure that your new hires include a bias toward those with an innovation focus and flair.

- *Involve with Integrity.* It is vital that people are given clear objectives and the broader context of the company's aims and ambitions. Only then can they really understand what is required to succeed. It is not enough to do this with centralized communications. Each manager and leader across the business must take the time to genuinely listen to their team members' ideas and help them to develop new products, services, and improvements that are in line with the company's priorities.

- *Provide Boundaries.* Empowerment does not happen in an organization without boundaries. On the contrary, a lack of boundaries can lead to paralysis where no one is sure about what is expected of them. Let people know what their limits are. These might include the types of products, services and improvements upon which you wish to focus, investment and funding ceilings and decision rights.

- *Drive Accountability.* Within these boundaries and objectives, give people full accountability for results. By giving them this freedom and responsibility, you will ensure that decisions are made as close as possible to the customer, rather than being driven back up the chain. It is vital that you don't always step in to prevent "failure." Such events are a critical part of your people's development and a necessary element of a way of working that will drive superior performance.

What opportunities do your people have to become involved in new, innovative projects, irrespective of their function?

Accelerator #6: Become the Market Leader at Innovation Partnerships

With most markets encountering rapidly changing technologies and customer tastes, it can pay to work with other organizations to develop new solutions and offers for several reasons. First, it is unlikely that you will have all the assets and capabilities you need to exploit any new opportunity, at least in the short term, so you will need to work with another organization that has those complementary skills. Second, you can reduce the risk from a new venture buy sharing investments. Third, as a result, you can use partnerships as a chance to learn more about a new market before making a more strategic outlay.

High-technology industries have embraced the need for collaboration in product development for a couple of decades at least, often in broader coalitions rather than simply as an arrangement between two of the players. This approach is now being replicated in other industries. Citroen, Peugeot, and Fiat, for example, combined their resources to produce their people carriers. The body and chassis of their different brands are the same; it is only the internal fit-out that changes. Similarly, if you wish to enter new, high-growth markets such as China and India, you will have no choice but to partner with a local company, but such a move can pay dividends in other countries as well, giving you access to local knowledge and relationships, at least in the early stages of your expansion.

Where are you using the power of partnerships to drive greater innovation and growth for your business, and what further opportunities do you have to build further partnerships and alliances that can benefit your customers and drive your innovation agenda?

Accelerator #7: Spend Real Time Observing Your Customers, Not Just Reviewing Reports

I have found that there is an inverse relationship between the length of a customer research report and the quality of its insights. As the report's number of pages increases, the chances of finding any nugget that could lead to real action and new benefits decreases proportionately. The trouble is that most customer research documents that I see are over 100 pages long! It's as if the researchers, painfully aware that their questions have failed to uncover anything worthwhile, try to confuse their buyers with excessive, and often contrary, statistics.

You cannot get a feel for what makes your customers tick, and what their real issues and unmet needs are, through the pages of a PowerPoint® pack. More direct involvement is required if you are to really understand what drives the people that you hope will buy your product or service. Companies of all shapes and sizes argue that they are customer-focused. However, putting customers at the heart of your innovation strategy requires moving beyond a two-dimensional un-derstanding of research reports to a deeper, three-dimensional level of knowledge and demands that managers from across the business get far closer to their buyers. This can involve observing customers in their normal, everyday surroundings, identifying issues and opportunities to take back to the business to work on, observing how customers shop for, buy and consume your product or simply spending time in your customers' shoes. Even if you are focused on internal clients, direct experience of your offering can bring home to you the realities of what it's like being your customer. Only when you've been standing in a retail store's queue with a screaming baby, or perhaps have tried to use your call center to ask for support, do you get an unfettered view of your customer experience.

How well do you combine formal research with direct and systematic management interaction with your customers?

Accelerator #8: Reward Behaviors, Not Just Results

I have already written that some level of failure is an intrinsic element of fast-lane innovation. Ensure that you support this reality by rewarding those that behave in ways that are likely to lead to innovation, even if not everything they have tried and developed has succeeded. Here are three practical ways you can do this:

1. **Focus Management Reports on the Quantity of Ideas, Not Just Their Quality.** It's generally accepted that best management prac-tice is to focus on outputs and outcomes, rather than inputs. That makes sense in normal circumstances, but not when you're trying to change behaviors. In those situations, you need to focus on inputs. So, instead of merely reviewing the value of your innovation pipe-line, report and review the number of ideas that have been created, have received funding for initial prototypes, have been selected for wider trials and testing, and have had the green light for full imple-mentation. And, if you also set goals and targets for these inputs, and embed them in relevant teams' performance contracts, you will start to see the new behaviors you're after.

2. **Celebrate Your Organization's Failures.** Governments may choose to bury bad news to avoid criticism, but if you fail to learn from your mistakes, and are unwilling to share the lessons with others, you are little better than the blue bottles constantly buzzing into a window when there is an open window just inches away. This means rewarding behaviors, not just profits. Why not have an awards ceremony each year when you not only recognize the new commercial successes, but where you also have categories such as "most glorious failure," "the very-nearly-but-not-quite-a-success," "the single biggest innovation lesson of the year," and "the most entrepreneurial manager?"

3. **Create Stories About People with the Right Stuff.** Stories resonate with people far more than statistics. Talking about those colleagues and managers who have demonstrated speed, tenacity, creativity, and leadership is worth a thousand bar charts and vision statements. Turning the people with the right behaviors into heroes will help show others what success really looks like. At M&S, one of Sir Stuart Rose's first actions as CEO was to share a story about how product manager designed, developed, and implemented a new line within a week, following Rose's criticism of the range. That story was used to show other managers that speed and action were at the core of the new management regime.

To what extent do you reward behaviors rather than successes, and what steps can you take to reward people who have actively sought to drive new innovations even if they haven't been totally successful?

CHAPTER 6

Implementing at Pace

The Speed of Light at the Center of the Sun

It takes a photon of light a little over 8 minutes to reach the earth after it leaves the sun's surface. In the vacuum of space, the photon literally travels at the speed of light over the 150-million-kilometer journey. But doesn't light always travel at that velocity? Well, not quite, as it turns out.

The center of the sun is incredibly densely packed with hydrogen and helium atoms—even more densely packed than shoppers at Macy's at the start of the seasonal sale!—and this means that the photon cannot escape quickly at all. Each photon's energy is repeatedly absorbed and released by these atoms, creating a path of travel that scientists call a "drunkard's walk" of 700,000 km through the center of the sun, rather than a straight line between the sun's core and its surface.

In probably the longest "drunkard's walk" ever, each photon takes 20,000 years or more (some estimates put it at 1 million years) traveling inside sun before starting its journey through space. It seems that the speed of light in the center of the sun slows down to 3 m per hour, less than the speed at which a snail crawls!

Why do I tell you this? Well, many business leaders highlight the need for pace when they really mean that they want their organization to do more. In a bid to raise performance, they add further initiatives, projects, and demands on managers and teams that are already struggling to deliver last month's priorities. As one strategic initiative hits all the other "special" projects—never mind "business as usual" operations—it loses momentum and slows down in a similar way to photons at the sun's core. Over time, each initiative performs its own "drunkard's walk," sometimes hitting a milestone and other times veering a million miles away from its goals and targets.

If you repeatedly try to launch too many projects at any one time, the "drunkard's walk" becomes almost inevitable. As the adage goes, "if everything is a priority, then nothing is a priority" and you simply end up in a situation where leaders can't lead, managers can't deliver and front-line teams become confused, fatigued, and dejected. I once spoke with a CEO who proudly told me that he had established 27 priorities for his company. When I asked him to name them, he struggled to get past 6 or 7 and gave up when he finally remembered Priority #9. If the CEO is unable to remember two-thirds of his priorities, what chance do the rest of the company's managers and workers have? A critical aspect of leadership is having a crystal clear message that you can communicate and reinforce regularly with your people. If you can't remember that message, you can't communicate it; and if you can't communicate it, your organization has next to no chance of delivering it. Many turnaround strategies start with a culling of the existing strategic agenda in a bid to create focus, energy, and pace around what's really important. In 2004, when Stuart Rose became CEO of U.K. retailer, M&S, for example, he quickly became aware of the problems created by the company's 31 strategic projects, rapidly reducing them to 10 mission critical initiatives.

In short, the desire for pace and progress can, paradoxically, create slower, less effective organizations. Although each project, on its own, has the potential to move rapidly and drive performance, collectively they end up colliding, canceling out each other's energy, and creating a gravitational pull from which they can't escape. So, what's the answer? There are four critical implementation boosters that can enable organizations to move from this cycle of decline and enter into an orbit of success:

1. **Focus, Focus, Focus.** Pace isn't about trying to do everything at once; it's about focusing your resources and energy on delivering against your most important issues and opportunities. Prioritization is a critical enabler of pace, and there is a clear correlation between those companies that are able to focus and those that move and deliver at speed.

2. **Lead by Results.** Developing great plans is all well and good, but real implementation pace, and achieving more things quicker and better than your competitors, is about taking prudent risks, having a

bias for action, and maintaining a focus on delivering tangible results and success.

3. **Think Big, Start Small.** Pace is not about being reckless or taking unnecessary risks, but about learning as cheaply and rapidly as possible so that you can invest in your success with as much confidence as possible. There is a clear sequence to follow when delivering new strategic initiatives, and those companies that choose to miss out critical steps do so at their peril.

4. **Remember, Delivery is the Day Job.** A key differentiator between those companies that are "first and fast" and those that are left in their wake is that the successful businesses are able to combine strategic progress with daily operational management. Their leaders know that delivery of the company's key strategic actions is just as much the day job as delivering against each customer order, and the companies that succeed most are those that are able to integrate these potentially competing priorities.

Let's look at each of these boosters in turn.

Focus, Focus, Focus: You Can't Chase Two Hares

One of the first actions Stuart Rose took when he became CEO of M&S was to reduce the number of "strategic initiatives" from 31 to 10. Rose's aim was to highlight to the entire business what was critical and what was irrelevant. He also highlighted the need for focus by creating three phases to the recovery of the business. The first phase, *Refocusing the Business*, concentrated on reducing costs, improving range, and providing better value for customers. The second phase, *Driving the Business*, began one year later, and set about improving the shopping environment and ensuring better customer service and was then followed by Phase 3, *Expanding the Business*, which aimed to deliver international growth, a multichannel offer, and new category development. The initial phases were more successful than the latter, but the message was clear: first things first.

There is a clear correlation between strategic focus and the pace of delivery. As we have seen, pursuing multiple goals means that you are unlikely to devote the necessary time, energy, or resources to any of them to achieve the breakthroughs in performance that you're after. The Japanese put it slightly differently: *you can't chase two hares*. If a hunting dog chases one hare, it might have a 10 percent chance of catching it, but if it tries to chase two hares at once, its chances of success rapidly fall to zero. The dogs quickly learn that 10 percent is the way to go. In a similar way, shoals of fish, and many grazing animals of the African Savannah, group together in their thousands in an effort to confuse their predators by giving them too much choice. Unless the shark or lion focuses on one target at a time, it will simply have to forego lunch.

For example, a manufacturing client had been looking to accelerate growth for several years. Its managers had developed many ideas and a string of initiatives for growth, but lacked a clear goal or a coherent agenda for action. During our work together, the management team identified a new, stretching goal that could never be achieved through business as normal. A list of potential initiatives to bridge the gap was created, but as we reviewed the long list, it became apparent that the company did not have the capability to deliver them. In fact, a key reason that growth continued to stall was that the organization did not have the ability to deliver consistent quality and on-time delivery of its orders. As a result, the Managing Director and his executive team decided to focus the entire organization's efforts on improving the company's performance in quality, as measured by its "On-Time, In-Full" order delivery KPI. As the performance measures improved, the company found that customer complaints fell, as did the rate of customer defections, and the subsequent growth built the energy and belief of the business, enabling the company to reach its strategic goal faster than it had originally forecast.

It takes discipline, and quite a bit of courage, not to respond to every problem or opportunity that comes your way, but as Steve Jobs once said, "It's only by saying no that you concentrate on the things that are really important." With that in mind, here are five specific actions you can take to increase your ability to say no, to increase your focus on your most important priorities, and to accelerate the future growth of your business:

1. **Reduce the Number of "Special Projects" in Your Business.** Stuart Rose reduced the number of "strategic projects" from 31 to 10, and my client decided to focus on a single objective—"On-Time,

In-Full" order delivery—to kick-start and accelerate its growth strategy. In my experience, most companies have at least twice as many "strategic projects" as they can reasonably handle, even at normal pace. If you want to put some more dramatic acceleration behind your true priorities, then it's likely you'll need to reduce the number of big initiatives by two-thirds or more. Here's how you can do it:

- Remove and stop any strategic projects that do not massively and directly contribute to your #1 strategic goal.
- If you still have a long list, determine if there is any logical sequence to the remaining projects, and defer those that are dependent on the outcomes of earlier, "foundation" projects.
- For the remaining projects, review them in detail and break them down into sub-projects. Repeat the two steps above so that your initial focus is on only those actions that will both massively deliver against your #1 strategic goal and build a platform for further initiatives in the future.

2. **Establish Priorities Within Your Priorities—But Only If You Have To.** You may have political reasons why you don't want to immediately kill all the strategic initiatives you are pursuing. But even in this situation you can still ensure that your focus—and relevant resource allocation decisions—favors your real priorities. At one client, I spoke with the CEO about the fact that he had 15 strategic priorities and challenged him that this was far too many for him to pursue successfully. "I know," he replied, "but I'm only really interested in three of them. Having the others makes sure that all our senior managers feel responsible for a key strategic project, but I have ensured that my very best people are on my top three." I wouldn't recommend this approach if you don't need to do it, but it can be a relatively effective alternative if some projects are at a critical stage and it would do more harm than good to fully halt them.

3. **Ensure that Your Critical Priorities Have the Resources and Capabilities they Need to Succeed.** If you reduce the number of projects you should be better able to ensure that each remaining priority is fully and properly resourced. Financial resources are central to this prioritization, but effective resource management is not just a financial question. Critically, this includes having a project leader

who has the necessary technical, organizational, and leadership capabilities to drive the initiative and deliver rapid results. It also means that you and your senior team give the project the attention it deserves, ensuring that it has the best possible chance of internal support and ultimate success.

4. **Establish "Phases" to the Delivery of Your Strategic Agenda.** Just because you have chosen not to undertake a specific project now does not mean that you will never do it. Your organization needs to understand that you recognize all the initiatives that need to be done, even if they're not currently in progress. An effective way to signal your intent is to establish phases to the delivery of your strategic agenda. As we have seen, Stuart Rose set out three phases—Refocus The Business, Drive The Business, and Expand The Business—each with its own set of priorities to show the business the future direction of M&S.

5. **Ensure the Performance Goal and Delivery Milestones of Your Priorities are Well-Known Across the Organization.** By sharing the strategy, the priorities and the KPIs and milestones with the wider business—through line manager discussions, set piece events, and internal newsletters—all your teams will understand what's important and why. This shared understanding enables the executive team to gain the support of the entire company to accelerate progress and drive for rapid success.

Lead By Results: The Inverse Relationship Between Detailed Planning and Performance Management

The old business saying, "fail to plan and you plan to fail," exemplifies an implementation approach that creates inertia, risk aversion, and drag. Far from aiding implementation, this mind-set acts as a brake on speed and progress. Don't get me wrong, I'm not against some planning, and I think that detailed plans and professional project management is critical for many major infrastructure projects, such as new systems development. But if you allow the planning of customer offer development initiatives to be taken over by professional planners and project managers, you will never be able to lead your market. The desire to ensure that all possible points of integration are fully understood and catered for ahead of any implementation and the need to develop the perfect sequence of events prior to action often looks good on paper, but can never model future reality. It's simply a waste of time.

If we return to where we started Chapter 1, at Nokia, the company's failure wasn't down to a lack of planning but to a lack of pace. Managers were trying to develop the perfect product—most likely based on perfect plans—which slowed product development down to a standstill at a time when Apple's iPhone, Android phones, and cheaper Chinese products were being launched onto the market, if not at the speed of light, then certainly faster than the speed of sound.

When it comes to creating and delivering a new or enhanced product or service, rather than the "fail to plan" mantra, I much prefer the military adage, "Plans rarely survive contact with the enemy" or, even better, Mike Tyson's quote that "everyone has a plan—'till they get punched in the mouth'!" Twenty-first century commercial success doesn't go to those companies that can plan the best, but to those that learn and adapt the quickest.

Figure 6.1 shows the difference between a planning-based approach to execution and an action-based approach. The lead times involved in detailed planning simply serve to inhibit progress. You are often able to run 10 or more rapid learning trials in the time it takes you to run a single, gold-plated, risk-adjusted trial. In the fully planned trial, you might be able to have a statistically robust sample of customers to test your ideas, but you're likely to find that you're simply too late to lead. Action-based implementation is iterative; it is based on an ongoing cycle of trial and error—with rapid follow-up.

The key point is this, though: the action-based approach works. At one retailer I worked with, management was looking at ways to improve in-store conversion and more compelling displays. With a planning-led approach, we would have taken a representative sample of customers, asked them lots of questions, identified key drivers of their behavior, designed a series of comprehensive (and expensive) store trials to test our emerging thinking, hired an agency to review customers' reaction to these improvements, and then refined our ideas before rolling out to other stores. The whole process could easily have taken more than a year and many thousands of pounds to complete, and we would have run

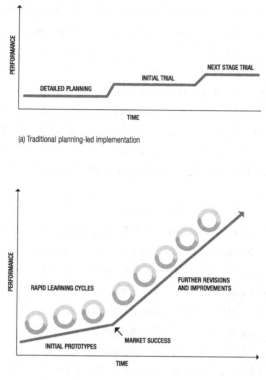

(a) Traditional planning-led implementation

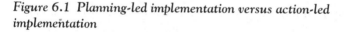

(b) Action-led implementation

Figure 6.1 Planning-led implementation versus action-led implementation

the risk of the initial trial not working and having to repeat the process. We took a different approach, however. In the space of three days, we identified 10 potential ideas to improve conversion, developed a series of "cardboard and string" prototypes and implemented them in store, and simply observed shoppers' behaviors. One of the ideas immediately hooked customers and within a few weeks had been implemented across the entire chain, growing both sales and customer satisfaction. A critical element of our success was getting the decision makers into the store, to help develop the ideas and even more importantly, to observe how the shoppers interacted with our various ideas. A couple of hours of watching real customers in action was worth a thousand research agency reports in terms of commitment to action.

That is why my favorite business quote of all time is this passage from *Bloomberg by Bloomberg*, the autobiography of Michael Bloomberg, the founder of the eponymous media and financial information empire: "We made mistakes of course. Most of them were omissions we didn't think of when we initially wrote the software. We fixed them by doing it over and over, again and again. We do the same today. While our competitors are still sucking their thumbs trying to make the design perfect, we're already on prototype version No. 5. By the time our rivals are ready with wires and screws, we are on version No. 10. It gets back to planning versus action. We act from day one; others plan how to plan—for months."

The planning-led approach that is endemic in many large organizations cripples their ability to move quickly to address new threats and opportunities. In fact, there is an inverse relationship between an organization's ability to deliver detailed operational plans and its ability to manage performance effectively, which I have seen over and over again in different businesses. The management teams that are effective at planning are rarely able to manage performance either quickly or effectively. The need for precision, cast-iron results and the unwillingness to take prudent risks means that they cannot quickly change the scope of a new initiative or exploit new opportunities and manage emerging threats as they arise. And that, in the end, is what happened at Nokia.

Figure 6.2 highlights the differences in skills, systems, organization, and culture between the requirements of an effective detailed planning focus and an effective performance management focus. The needs of these two approaches are, in general, mutually exclusive. Take the organizational approach, for example. If you want your business to have a higher level of planning capability, you will need to increase the level of centralized control and coordination so that you can embed standardized approaches to work and also ensure that all the major risks points of possible integration have been identified and planned for up-front. Conversely, if you want to develop improved levels of performance management and a higher focus on results, you will seek to devolve accountability to front-line managers and challenge them to find the best way to drive improvements. Now, you may be saying to yourself that you want the best of both: to have effective planning and excellence in managing and improving performance.

PLANNING FOCUS		PERFORMANCE FOCUS
Planning and risk management	KEY SKILLS	Action-based learning
Delivery against the timeline	MANAGEMENT FOCUS	Customer and Financial results
Central co-ordination	ORGANIZATIONAL APPROACH	Devolved Accountability
Weekly progress review meetings	ROUTINES AND RITUALS	Site reviews of the latest prototype solution
"Control and co-ordination will deliver success"	UNDERLYING BELIEFS	"The faster we act, the faster we learn and the faster we succeed"

Figure 6.2 The inverse relationship between detailed planning and performance management

But you can't square a circle. When you try to balance the two approaches, you simply create huge tensions in your company between the planners and the doers, leading to widespread frustration and paralysis. In the end you, will have to choose. And my strong advice to you is to err on the side of action and performance management.

Think Big, Start Small: Tesco Express Versus Fresh & Easy

In September 2013, Tesco, the world's third largest grocer, agreed to hand over Fresh & Easy, its loss-making U.S. chain, to the private equity firm, Yucaipa. Rather than receiving cash for the sale, the disposal cost Tesco over $200 million. This cost merely added to the $1.5 billion cumulative losses that had already been racked up by the embryonic chain following its launch in 2007. Tesco's previous international expansion had not always been plain sailing—it had sold loss-making subsidiaries in South Korea and Japan, for example—but the U.S. investment was its most costly by far.

What made the huge losses so baffling to me was the fact that the grocer had previously demonstrated a willingness to adopt a "learn-by-doing" approach to its international and new business development activities rather than the "silver bullet" approach it used with Fresh & Easy. For example, when the company developed a new convenience store format, Tesco Express, in the 1990s, it did so in clear stages. Management started small, they then, through a series of trial stores learned as quickly as they could about this new convenience format, and only then did they fire the main rockets of investment. This was no overnight success. Having launched the first trial store in 1994, it took the company over six years to put 20 stores on the ground. This was the first of three phases of development.

- **1994–1999—Prove The Concept.** By 1999, there were 17 stores, and the Annual Report quietly noted that Tesco Express was becoming a "promising format." Behind the scenes, the format development team was busy developing and testing many different variants of the store, so that a model that was appealing to customers, operationally effective, and financially attractive could be rolled out. The end result of this concept development period was the announcement in 1999 of a joint venture with Esso, where Tesco Express stores would be introduced to more than 100 Esso gas stations.
- **1999–2003—Build Scale.** The deal with Esso created new store opportunities for Tesco. The 100 Esso stores that were added over the next four years enabled the Tesco Express format to reach a level of scale, delivering sales of up to $500 million. The format was ready for its next stage of development.
- **2003 onward—Accelerate Growth.** Having built a sustainable business, Tesco then set about accelerating the chain's growth and become the United Kingdom's convenience store market leader. Critical to this stage was Tesco's acquisition of the T&S Convenience stores chain, which they quickly rebranded to Tesco Express. Further deals

and stores openings followed this acquisition and by 2011 the company now had approximately 1,000 Tesco Express stores, delivering in the region of $5 billion in annual sales.

Could Tesco have gone faster with the early stages of development and condensed, for example, the initial, "Prove The Concept" phase in a couple of years rather than six? The answer is that they probably could. At the time, however, the company was focusing on maximizing the growth from its core chain of supermarkets and launching its larger format, Tesco Extra. But that initial stage was critical. It allowed management to understand what customers wanted from a convenience store and how best to create a profitable operating model. By having only a handful of stores, it was relatively easy for the development team to change the customer offer and test new ideas. They were not encumbered with the complexities and dynamics of running a full retail chain.

By contrast, the Fresh & Easy experience effectively missed out the "Prove The Concept" phase that was so vital to the success of Tesco Express. Instead, Tesco announced a move to the United States in 2006, following a year-long research program, led by the U.K. marketing director, who had spent a year in the Southwest states of California, Nevada, and Arizona, understanding customer needs and shopping habits so that the business could create a distinctive and attractive neighborhood grocery store.

Unfortunately, this intensive research program didn't work. A rapid and immediate expansion of the chain meant that, despite the initial research, the company effectively planted the new format in the United States and then had to hope that it would work first time—the exact opposite of what the CEO had claimed! Within two years, there were over 100 branches in the chain. In addition, the company had invested in a 1.4 million square foot distribution center in Riverside County, California. Not only was this a sign of commitment to the Fresh & Easy concept, but it was also a significant and visible fixed cost, raising the stakes even further.

Unsurprisingly, problems with the Fresh & Easy offer quickly began to emerge, including the following:

- The focus on self-checkout aisles was seen as less convenient to U.S. shoppers who preferred having sales assistants scan through their items.

- The limited in-store range prevented the chain from carrying some well-known brands.
- The stores offered a uniform assortment and didn't customize merchandise by neighborhood.
- The grocer pre-packed vegetables, as they did in the United Kingdom, even though the U.S. shopper preferred to buy fruits and vegetables from loose displays.

What's more, in 2008, the U.S. economy shrank into a recession that badly hit the high-growth cities and neighborhoods that Tesco was targeting. In late 2010, the management team decided to "mothball" 13 stores, particularly those in Las Vegas and Phoenix that were suffering from declining housing and labor markets. At the time, the company said that it would focus on further store openings "around coastal California" and other areas where the economy had been less severely hit.

Even so, by 2010 there were 170 stores and the chain continued to expand. The relatively poor performance of the stores continued, resulting in annual losses of around $200 to 300 million per annum and the eventual decision of the group board to close the chain and dispose of it. To an outside observer, it seemed that the Fresh & Easy management team was playing a high-risk game of "double or quits." To each piece of bad news, management attached a new growth and expansion goal that tied them to focusing on adding stores rather than improving performance of the existing stores.

Tesco's management had, in effect, taken the opposite approach that had worked so well for Tesco Express. Instead of starting small, learning fast and then firing the main rockets, they had fired the main rockets immediately, started big and then failed to learn very much at all. This book is all about taking prudent risks to drive pace in your business so that you can lead your markets. But there is a clear difference between pace and haste. If you try to reach top speed immediately, without going through the gears, you will simply stall—even Usain Bolt doesn't reach top speed until 50 m in a 100-m race—and that is exactly what happened to Tesco's Fresh & Easy concept, as shown in Figure 6.3.

Starting small may seem counterintuitive to pace, but it is in fact fundamental. If you focus on a single product, factory, store, team or region, rather than taking on your entire organization, you can learn far faster.

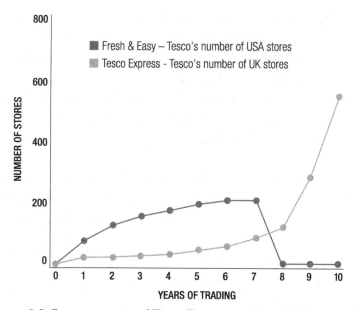

Figure 6.3 Store expansion of Tesco Express and Fresh & Easy in the first 10 years

You have the ability to change things on a Monday and see how it's gone on a Friday. I know from experience that if I attempted to test a new idea or initiative in 20 stores, it simply became a logistical, rather than learning, exercise. There would simply be too many people involved to be able to make the tweaks and ad hoc improvements necessary to go from initial prototype to fully developed concept.

What's more, starting small doesn't mean limiting your ambition. On the contrary, if you narrow the scope of your implementation, you can raise your performance aspirations. One client, for example, was looking to reduce their level of warehouse stock across their distribution chain. By focusing on a single distribution center, we were able to develop a far more ambitious goal—reducing stock by 50 percent—than we could possibly have done if we'd started with five or ten centers. This focus on a single center and ambitious goal gave the warehouse team the incentive and leeway to be both creative and experimental and, within a couple of months, new approaches had been developed that were then implemented across the wider organization.

Starting small gives you the ability to learn fast and to then have confidence to fire the investment rockets. It is what drove the success of Tesco Express and its absence from the Fresh & Easy implementation was at the heart of this concept's failure.

Remember, Delivery is the Day Job: The Secret to Rapid Transformation

Over 60 percent of corporate transformation programs fail to achieve their goals. Not only is this a huge waste of financial resources and human effort, but it also makes future success less likely. Your ability to persuade your organization to commit to your new strategic transformation is radically reduced when your people have literally read the book, seen the film and bought—or been given—the t-shirt, mug, and mousepad. Simply put, transformation programs slow companies down in both the short and long term.

A key issue is that transformation programs are created and designed by corporate office teams in the company's headquarters. The solutions they develop are often grounded in what seems to be sound analysis, and their implementation plans make sense at the launch of the program. The problems are that the front-line teams have many priorities they must deliver and that things change rapidly both within a business, its markets and its competitors. Unfortunately, too few of these top-down programs have the built-in flexibility to cope with these new realities, creating tensions across the organization and a failure to match resources to results.

Instead of building common ground across an organization, top-down transformation programs build battlegrounds, reducing both speed and performance. A different approach is needed to drive speed and results, and it starts with integrating your transformation goals with everyone's daily responsibilities so that delivery becomes the day job. Legions of research projects have shown that people perform better at work when they feel in control. Autonomy is a prerequisite of high performance and is at the heart of implementing at pace.

But how do you have autonomy without anarchy? How do you combine autonomy with accountability? The key is to align your key corporate goals with both team and individual goals. That way you enable your people to buy into the goals, contribute to their delivery, and accelerate progress. There are three fundamental steps you need to take:

Step 1: Determine Everyone's #1 Goal

The first step to integrating your change or transformation agenda and people's day job is to agree to the specific goals for each of your teams and managers. Wherever possible, these should be fully aligned with your #1 goal (see Chapter 3). At one manufacturer to the building industry, for example, the executive team had agreed a #1 goal of becoming their industry's leader for customer loyalty. As they cascaded this goal across the business, the functional goals that were developed and agreed included the following:

- Each factory established a #1 goal focused on "on-time, in-full" delivery of customer orders.
- Sales teams developed and managed a "Net Promoter Score" set of goals, by region, to ensure that their account teams were building lasting relationships and not just pushing sales.
- The delivery teams established a #1 goal of improving the reliability of delivery against forecast time slots (which had been raised as a key issue by their customers).
- The finance team set itself a #1 goal of having a single, on-time invoice for each transaction with the customer within 24 hours of delivery (again, multiple and late invoices had been a source of irritation for customers).
- The purchasing team agreed a #1 goal of working with the company's suppliers to reduce the lead time for order delivery so that the business could become more responsive to special orders.

Each functional goal was different, but they all contributed to the overall #1 goal. Equally, the goals did not clash with each other. On the contrary, they were mutually supportive. The purchasing team's goal, for example, helped the factories to improve their level of on-time production, and the finance team's top goal enabled the sales teams to have more positive meetings with customers.

Each function further cascaded the goals they had developed to subteams and individuals so that accountability was held in the most appropriate place. Where there was little alignment between a team's activity and the #1 goal—for example, in the payroll department—alternative productivity goals were set, but these were not allowed to cut across or distract from other teams' focus on delivering the company's #1 goal.

Finally, all goals were also specifically quantified: there was a number attached to each goal. Each team was then able to identify when the goal had been met and what progress looked like. Success was black or white, enabling managers to take full control of their results and performance.

Step 2: Allow Your Teams to Determine the Actions Required

Although you need to ensure that each team's goal is directly driving your overall #1 goal, it is essential that every team takes ownership of what needs to be done to achieve that goal. If they are told what to do, as is the case in many transformation programs, you will simply end up with resistance and delay. As long as the goals are aligned and integrated, the actions should follow.

The finance team of the building products manufacturer, for example, spent 8 weeks redesigning its processes and redistributing the responsibilities of certain members of their team. They also demanded and gained agreement to certain changes in the content and format of information that was provided by the sales representatives and by the production department. These improvements enabled the team to step change the accuracy and speed of their invoices, reducing customer queries and complaints and improving the company's cash flow. There had been no need for a formal, centrally controlled project—the finance team's managers and colleagues had simply responded to the goal that they had helped develop and integrated the actions required into their daily and weekly activities.

By providing autonomy and accountability to the relevant function, you will not only benefit from faster performance improvement, you can also gain extra improvement as a result of using ideas that you would never have identified or considered through a central team. At one fur-niture retailer, delivery teams were asked by management to improve the level of customer satisfaction from their service. At one depot, the various teams had a meeting to come up with improvement ideas. One idea was to ask the householder for their vacuum cleaner and to offer to clean up any bits and pieces that were left behind from the packaging.

A delivery team comprising some young, enthusiastic colleagues de-cided to use this idea. A separate team, staffed with older, more cynical colleagues, told them that this was a waste time. At the end of the first week, the wider group came together again. Not only had the young de-livery team seen their satisfaction scores go through the roof, they also had over £200 in tips from their happy customers. What's more, most customers didn't even get their vacuum cleaner out; they were simply astounded that any delivery team would even offer to clean up after them-selves. Unsurprisingly, within a few weeks, even the older, cynical delivery team had begun to offer vacuum cleaning services to their customers. A mix of autonomy and accountability had rapidly accelerated perfor-mance improvement and built long-lasting engagement and commitment to the company's strategy and priorities in a way that a centrally con-trolled program could never have achieved.

Some activities, of course, require working across functions to corpo-rately agreed priorities. Implementing a new IT system or developing new products requires individual departments and teams to work with other departments as part of a wider activity plan. In these instances, there has to be commitment to the wider corporate effort. Even here, however, it's possible to provide each team some leeway as to how they get the job done, and wherever this opportunity arises, it is in your company's best interest to take it.

Step 3: Establish and Embed Performance Management Disciplines

The third and final step to align transformation and the day job is to establish and embed performance management disciplines within each team. The metrics measured must specifically include their #1 goal, but there may be more metrics that the teams track, particularly where the goal is likely to require a long-term effort. At one office cleaning business, for instance, the innovation team had a specific goal relating to sales from new products. The first of these products would not be available for sale for at least six months, however. Consequently, the team began to track some related measures that were aligned to their longer-term goal. These metrics included the level of training of the sales and technical service teams in the new products, their level of commitment and belief in the new range, and an audit of the logistical capabilities of each of their geographical markets to supply the new products. By improving the scores of these metrics in the intervening six months, the innovation team was able to hit their sales targets after several years of mediocre performance from new product launches.

Your teams should manage performance against their goal themselves, but, equally, they should be willing to share progress with others. Some teams create highly visual charts that they hang in meeting rooms or communal areas as a way of visualizing progress and maximizing involvement. Other teams either invite or are invited to attend regular sessions with top management. Whatever specific approaches you use, the key to your company's success will be your ability to embed these reviews so that managers, teams, and colleagues feel responsible and accountable for results and that they have the ongoing autonomy to make the necessary changes and improvements to their plans so that they hit their goals as quickly and as effectively as possible.

CHAPTER 7

Allowing Your Customers to Navigate

Steve Jobs was An Error: The Customer's Not Always Right, But That's the Way to Bet

In dynamic, turbulent, and fast-moving markets, driven by almost unbelievable technological advancements, you can easily become distracted by the noise and activity in your markets and forget this critical business truth. You do so at your peril. Like a party of trekkers in the Himalayas who stay physically close to their guides during the raging storms that can descend unexpectedly in the mountains, you need to stay close to your customers at all times. They can guide your next steps and help lead you to a successful outcome. Customers may not set your destination or the mountain you choose to climb, but they can provide the necessary navigation to help you arrive safely—if you let them.

So far, so obvious, but how many companies stay close enough to their customers, listen hard enough to their customers, and act quickly enough on the guidance they're given, to enable them to either lead their markets or at least move faster than their competitors? In my experience, the answer is remarkably few. Even huge organizations with seemingly bottomless marketing budgets can spectacularly fail to respond to their customers' changing needs and wants. That is what, in part, happened at Nokia. The company was not short of market research insights, but even if the management heard the message that mobile phone buyers preferred new, competitor products, they were unable or unwilling to act upon it.

The rival that first dented Nokia's dominance was Apple, led by its founder, Steve Jobs. Jobs was famous for eschewing market research, preferring to rely on his own instincts to determine what customers should or should not be offered. As a result, other CEOs are able to point at one of the world's most successful companies and tell themselves that Apple is a model they should follow. Don't rely on customers to tell you which way to go next, they say, but trust your own judgment and they will then follow. This is a dangerous approach to take, for three key reasons.

1. **Steve Jobs was An Error.** By that I mean that he was a freak, a genius. Trying to emulate Steve Jobs's idiosyncratic—and often unbelievably frustrating—management style is as likely to succeed for you as an artist is to succeed by trying to emulate Michelangelo. Jobs had grown up playing with and developing computers. He intimately understood their possibilities and their shortcomings, and, as a result, was able to intuitively feel what was likely to work next. When he saw the Graphical User Interface—or mouse—being demonstrated at HP's Palo Alto development center, he immediately realized its potential and likely success, and was determined to link it to his Macintosh computer. He didn't need market research to tell him, because he was the embodiment of the Apple customer; he was his company's own research panel. It is unusual for a CEO to be so embedded in the detail of the products and services sold by the company they lead. Without that intimate knowledge, your ability to use your gut feel and intuition to lead the development of your customer offer is completely flawed.

2. **Steve Jobs Worked in a Frontier Industry.** In the 1980s, the personal computer market didn't really exist. Aside from a few fanatics in California, there was little corporate interest in developing computers that would be used in people's homes. The money was focused on large corporate machines, and IBM was the clear market leader. Steve Jobs at Apple and Bill Gates and his team at Microsoft were both critical in creating the personal computer market. Without them, the market would have developed more slowly and very differently. The personal computer market was a frontier industry; there were no rules to tell you what to do, and no existing customers to tell you what improvements to make. Relying on customer feedback was not, therefore, an option. When Jobs returned to Apple and developed iTunes, the iPod, and the iPhone, he was similarly attracted

to nascent markets with little consumer guidance. Most markets are not like those that Jobs played in. Most markets are either already pretty well developed or have at least evolved from existing markets. Michael O'Leary at Ryanair, for instance, may have revolutionized the European airline market, but he was able to learn the model and the key consumer lessons from Southwest Airline's experience in the United States. You too are likely to be involved in established markets and so have the advantage of talking to existing customers about their preferences and frustrations. It is an advantage you should use.

3. **Steve Jobs was Misunderstood.** Jobs wasn't against customer feedback and research *per se*; he was against asking customers to predict how they would respond to something that hadn't been created. He worked in a market with nonincremental developments. Consumers are notoriously bad at predicting their own future behavior, and so Jobs didn't bother to ask them. In the early days of Apple, as he admitted himself, he knew most of his potential market personally— they were at the same computer club that he attended—and so he was able to develop products that he believed would have a reasonable chance of meeting their needs. Even as Apple began to grow and develop, he would share emerging developments with potential customers to see if the new potential offering was likely to receive a warm reception. In an interview as far back as 1990, for example, he said, "Once you've made that jump is a great time to go check your instincts with the market place and verify that you're on the right track." In other words, Jobs wasn't going to let his target customers grab hold of the steering wheel of his developments, but he would allow them to provide navigational feedback and guidance so that he could make the necessary adjustments to the direction of travel.

It's true that your customers aren't always able to give you the correct answer about their future behavior. They may tell you that they'll turn left in a certain situation, only to turn right when that situation actually happens. I remember, for example, once reading some customer research that concluded that a retailer's customers would visit the store more often if a particular new service was introduced, only for shopper numbers to continue to decline following its implementation. It is far more common, however, for your sales and profitability to accelerate and your market position to improve if you are able tap into the needs and wants of your customers in a more committed, systematic way. And, despite the myths that have built up around Steve Jobs, this is what Apple's founder achieved in a way that suited the company's culture and its markets.

Who to Implore and Who to Ignore

Not all customers are created equal. Listening to some customers can transform the growth of your business, while paying the same amount of attention to other customer groups can significantly impede progress. It is critical therefore that you are clear about which customers you are working with to help navigate your company's performance. Get it right and you will be sailing smoothly to your destination; but get it wrong and you may find yourself beached on the reefs and rocks of your market's shallower waters, or battling storms that you hadn't seen coming and for which you had not prepared.

In fact, there are just four key customer groups that you need to really get to know and understand. If you can work effectively with these customers, you will significantly raise your chances of steering your business through whatever turbulence the market throws your way. Let's look at each in turn:

1. **Your Most Valuable Customers.** These customers are the focus of most management teams. It is common that an 80/20 situation exists, where approximately 20 percent of your customer base will deliver around 80 percent of your company's revenues, and an even higher share of your business's profits. Maintaining and enhancing your share of these customers' business is critical to its ongoing health and success. Consequently, and unsurprisingly, many retail, consumer, and business-to-business companies run reward and loyalty schemes—whether that's in the form of discounts, rebates, points or gifts, and events—to keep this critical group of customers happy. So far, so obvious, but the key aspect of working with these customers to help navigate your future success is, as we shall see below, to understand when you need to listen to them above

all other customer groups, and when to put other customer groups' opinions ahead of theirs.

2. **Other High-Value Customers in Your Market.** It is less common for businesses to pay close attention to these customers. Yet the 80/20 principles that apply to your own revenues are just as relevant to the market as a whole. Finding and understanding the needs and desires of the 20 percent of customers that drive the overall value of your market is equally important as understanding the perceptions of your existing best customers. Some of your top customers may already be in this group, but they may not be representative of the total opinion of this critical segment. When the executive team of one consumer goods business I worked with realized that they only had a 15 percent share of their core markets' top customers, and that they had focused too much of their attention and resources on their existing most valuable customers, they quickly changed their goals to growing their share of the market's top customers. This move led to new product and service innovations that both attracted new customers and delighted and grew their existing top consumers.

3. **Your Other Existing Customers.** This group is the flip side of the first segment; it is the remaining 80 percent of your customers that will contribute around 20 percent of your revenues. Again, some of these customers may be high-value customers in your market, but just not buy that much from your company, but the majority are likely to be relatively low value in the market as a whole. In my experience, these are the customers that are most focused on low prices and bargains and, unless you are pursuing a strategy of being the price leader in your market, it is likely that you will be overly focused on this group. It's not that you ignore this group, but that you need to put their views into perspective. Even if you did everything they were after, it is unlikely that they will repay you with massive sales growth. It is these customers that can act as a strategic distraction for managers. They represent a large number of buyers but are simply not valuable enough to drive your future success.

4. **Your Market's Innovators and Early Adopters.** The final group is, in most markets, a relatively small number of customers. Yet, in dynamic and turbulent markets, they can act as a critical guide to

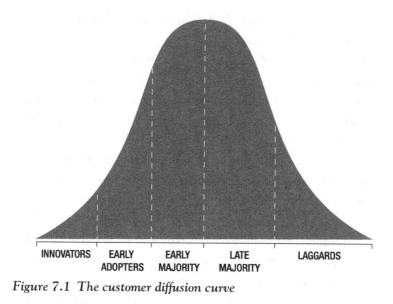

| INNOVATORS | EARLY ADOPTERS | EARLY MAJORITY | LATE MAJORITY | LAGGARDS |

Figure 7.1 The customer diffusion curve

new tastes, new demands, and likely future successes. As shown in the customer diffusion curve in Figure 7.1, "innovators" and "early adopters" first buy new innovations before the majority of more conservative buyers are willing to accept them. In mature markets, the decline of most incumbents is that they fail to pay sufficient attention to this group and remain solely focused on the needs of their best customers. As the diffusion curve of a radical new innovation or a new disruptive player in the market spreads to the majority of customers in the market, it becomes too late for the incumbents to change and their position in the market rapidly declines. That is what happened, in large part, to Nokia and a similar pattern is evident, for example, in the airline market, where cheap, low-fare competitors have overtaken the major players. Not all innovations, of course, make it past the small group of innovators or early adopters in the diffusion curve—think of Sony's MiniDisc, for instance—but it is better to pay more, rather than less attention to this group if you are to stay on top of the dynamic changes in your market and the future shifts in the tastes and preferences of your best customers. This group of innovators and early adopters can act as an early warning system within your overall navigational approach, and are critical to your ongoing success.

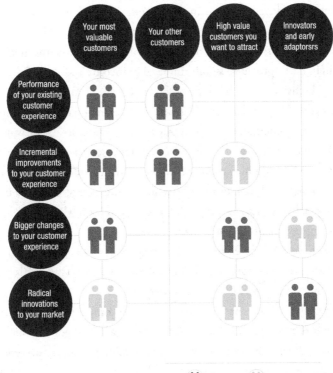

Figure 7.2 When to listen to different customer groups

It is vital that you seek out the views and opinions of all four of these groups, and even within these groups you will need to further segment the customers to really understand what's driving the differences in opinions and behaviors. Only then can you continue to craft your strategy, your brand, and your products and services to ensure that you remain relevant to your target customers. But while you need to maintain a general measurement of all four groups, the relative importance of these different market segments varies according to the decision you are seeking to make. As Figure 7.2 describes, while some groups are critical to certain decisions, they can be a distraction to making other types of decisions.

In terms of the ongoing delivery and continuous improvement of your existing, core customer offer, for instance, you need to be hardwired into the feedback from your existing customers. Your top customer group in this situation is your most valuable customers. You need to ensure that you keep their loyalty and business, and respond rapidly to the problems and issues they have. The second most important group is your other existing customers. Although not as valuable as your top customers, they are still likely to provide a significant level of income and should therefore need to be listened to and understood if you are to keep their business. The customers who are highly valuable in your market but who are not your core customers are your third priority. In some cases, the reason they don't use you are highly strategic, but in other cases, they can be attracted by some tweaks and improvements to your existing offer. Innovators and early adopters are less relevant in this area as they are often bored by the everyday delivery of an existing offer; their focus is on what's new, not on minor improvements to your existing offer.

When you are developing and testing bigger changes to your core offer, the relative importance of your different customer groups is different. While your most valuable customers are still your priority, the views of other valuable customers in your market become far more important, as they are more likely to be attracted by bigger changes to your offer. Correspondingly, the views of your less valuable customers become less important as it is unlikely that they will have the buying power to deliver against your growth ambitions.

Finally, when you are considering radical innovation that will offer something new and very different to your market, the views of innovators and early adopters become the most important customer group. Back in the summer of 1989, for instance, a group of senior managers from Renault were reviewing the customer research for a proposed new small car. The car was completely different from anything else in the market—the front end of the design was completely unconventional, resembling a smiley face, and all the interior equipment was raised on a central console to free space—and, as a result, the market research had delivered mixed results. While around 20 percent of those tested loved the new design, over half hated it. Some marketing managers raised the idea of tweaking the design to make it more acceptable to the majority of target customers, but the lead designer, Patrick Le Quément insisted that the design should go ahead without any further amendments from focus groups. Following the meeting he wrote to Renault's president, Raymond Levy, saying, "The biggest risk for us is not to take any risk. I ask you to choose an instinctive design rather than extinctive marketing." Levy ended up supporting Le Quément and the new car, named the Twingo, went on to become one of the most successful launches in European car history. Renault's executive team had delivered a game-changing design by focusing its attention and its decision making on innovative and early-adopting customers and paying less attention to the mass of more conservative customers, who were not, at that stage, open to the car's advantages.

How to Work with Customers to Accelerate Innovation

Winning the race to develop and offer new solutions for customers is at the heart of 21st-century business success. And, just as we need to think differently about how companies organize internally to meet this challenge, we also need to think differently about how we engage and work with customers. Here are six ways that you can get better and faster insights from your customers so that you become the fastest, and ultimately the first, in your market.

1. **Talk to the Right Customers.** As we've already discussed, not all customers are the same. When dealing with new products and services, you need to talk to customers who are more accepting and welcoming of innovations. From Figure 7.2, it is the early adopters, in particular, that can often give the best indication of likely success. Innovators are likely to respond positively to anything that's new, but "early adopters" are more discerning and will take more convincing of your product's benefits before giving you a positive response.

    In short, the right customers to engage to drive your innovation process are not necessarily representative of your existing customer base as a whole. Instead, they are the ones who are best placed to understand what you're trying to achieve. They can act, in many ways, as a glimpse into the future, as the majority of customers may catch up with their tastes within the next year or two. These customers can also influence the mass-market consumers, as they are likely to be bloggers, opinion formers, and recommenders to more conservative buyers.

2. **Use the Right Environment.** Too much research takes place on the end of a phone line or e-mail connection or in faceless meeting

rooms. If you're a retailer, test your latest retail thinking in a store. If you're a restaurant, talk to your customers as they're eating a meal or at home making plans for the next meal out. The managers at Marriott hotels, for instance, realized that they were over-investing in their lobbies when they observed that guests seldom used the sofas or chairs that were freely available in these areas. When they engaged with their customers, they understood that waiting around in hotel lobbies was not something that people wanted to be seen doing. As a result, the development team spent more effort creating a database of recommended places to visit at each hotel, as that was something that their guests really valued. In other words, by focusing their research in real hotels, Marriott's managers were able to identify insights that customers would never have raised in a typical focus group conference room workshop.

3. **Prototypes, Not Concepts.** Focusing on your customers' actual decisions, rather than their unreliable predictions about those potential decisions, means that you should use prototypes in your research whenever possible. They then have the chance to play with the product or experience the service, rather than simply giving you reactions to what is likely to be an abstract concept. As we discussed earlier, Steve Jobs didn't necessarily ask customers what they wanted, but he strongly believed in going back to customers with prototypes and models to check that his new idea was likely to fit with what customers needed. Critically, the prototype does not need to be particularly advanced for it to help customers make the mental leap from an abstract notion to a concrete idea. For example, I once ran an idea generation workshop with a foot care company and we ended the day discussing some of our best ideas with a panel of target customers. One of the ideas we came up with was an exfoliating sock. The customers were having trouble understanding the concept, so one of the managers got hold of a normal sock and added some exfoliating lotion to the inside of it. He told the focus group that the product wouldn't be as "oily" as this prototype but that it would provide an exfoliating effect. One or two of the customers tried the sock on and instantly gave more vivid and richer feedback on what it would take to make it attractive enough for them to consider buying.

4. **The Power of Instant Feedback.** The use of a focus group at the end of an idea-generation workshop is an example of instant feedback. It provides far greater momentum into any new product or service development process than waiting weeks for more formal research. Critical to its success is that the developers need to be involved in the feedback process. That way the development team isn't relying on researcher's interpretations and reformulations of customers' responses, but they can actually witness user responses themselves, providing them with richer, more visceral and quicker information to use in the next stage of the development process. I have worked with the new offer development team of several retailers, for instance, where we have simply created an idea and implemented an initial, rapidly prototyped solution in-store and then observed shoppers to see if and how they interact with our new solution. The results are virtually immediate. If the first few shoppers fail to interact with a new display, no amount of waiting is likely to change that pattern. As a result, setting up prototypes in a way that gives you instant feedback can act as a huge accelerator on your new offer development process.

5. **Exploit Technology.** The use of technology can help you develop your ideas faster, but also get faster and better feedback and insights from your customers. In the digital world, for example, it is possible to rapidly develop prototype websites and apps that you can share with a sample of customers to gain views and check your thinking. Some major consumer goods companies that I work with have an entire virtual store that, with the aid of special goggles, people can shop and interact with prototyped virtual displays. These research centers can cost millions of dollars to develop, but you don't need to invest so much to exploit technology effectively. You can now ask your customers to use the video recorders on their smart phones to create a video diary of their thoughts and ideas, or to create a real-time video of their entire customer experience. Online questionnaires and customer panels can also enable you to gain rapid feedback on their thoughts and the use of social networks or group messenger apps can enable customers to share, pool, and develop insights and ideas with the development team.

6. **Co-creation Between Customers and Executives.** Not only can customers provide feedback on your ideas, but they can also become involved in their development. This happens most rapidly and most effectively when they are done alongside the development team. At one client, a customer development team worked with a small group of customers and one or two senior executives over a period of a few weeks to collectively develop some new product and service ideas. In the initial workshop, the customer group was dismissive of the team's concepts, complaining that they were insufficiently distinctive and were, in essence, me-too ideas. The development team went away and came back with more radical and distinctive ideas. These led to more constructive discussions in the subsequent meetings, and within four weeks, full-scale prototypes had been developed for wider and more detailed testing.

All six of these ideas are about getting your customers far more closely integrated with your innovation and product development processes and creating faster feedback loops so that you can refine and develop your ideas at pace. In some cases, this may take several months of work, but in others, as we have seen, you can reduce the development phase to a matter of days, enabling you to get ahead of your rivals and be the innovation leader of your market.

Customer Navigation in Action: Embedding Customer Focus at DFS

DFS is the United Kingdom's largest sofa retailer. Operating over 100 stores nationwide, the company generated profits of over £80 million in 2014 on turnover of a little over £800 million. Its brand and awareness has been developed over 45 years by major investment in TV advertising. Most U.K. consumers know DFS for its frequent sales events and its famous message that "this offer must end Sunday." They also know the retailer for its highly motivated commission-based store teams that are completely focused on selling.

In 2010, its founder, Lord Kirkham, sold DFS to Advent, a London-based private equity house. A new management team, led by Ian Filby, a veteran of U.K. retail giant, Boots the Chemists, refreshed the company's strategy to identify new avenues for growth. This strategy was highly challenging, particularly as the United Kingdom was still in the midst of its biggest recession since the 1930s. Filby and his team realized early in the process that the retailer needed to transform its customers' experience. Dwindling household budgets and the rise of discount competition, both on the high streets and retail parks of the United Kingdom, and through the web, meant that a hard sell approach could no longer work. Instead, the company had to earn the trust and loyalty of its customers, in addition to offering outstanding value for money.

Filby asked his HR Director, Andrew Stephenson, to lead this critical strategic initiative. Stephenson, who had previously worked in various operational roles for other U.K. retailers, including the home improvement giant B&Q, Dixons and Vodafone, worked rapidly with the rest of the senior team to develop a new customer experience model that focused on establishing a better understanding of customers' needs and working to meet those needs. The new experience model was implemented across the chain with a clear uplift in both customer satisfaction and sales. But Stephenson knew that these gains would, over time, be lost without ongoing measurement and management of the sales teams' behaviors. Consequently, he began to develop ways to embed a greater customer focus across the business every day.

At the heart of the new DFS approach was the use of the Net Promoter Score (NPS). First developed by Fred Reicheld of Bain Consulting, NPS, is an indicator of customer loyalty based around customer responses to a single question: *on a scale of 0 to 10 how likely are you to recommend [our company] to friends and family?* Those customers who rate your business 9 or 10 are called "promoters," while those who score 0 to 6 are deemed "detractors" as they are likely to complain about you to others. Customers who score 7 or 8 are called "passives," as they are likely to be reasonably satisfied with the experience you deliver, but not satisfied enough to recommend you to their friends and colleagues. Your NPS is then determined by subtracting the percentage of customers who are "detractors" from those who are "promoters." Your score could therefore fall anywhere between −100 percent and +100 percent, although it is generally recognized that scores of 50 percent or more are associated with companies that deliver a consistently excellent customer experience.

On the back of some effective marketing, and despite some academic criticism about its superiority to other customer satisfaction measures, NPS has become a common metric in many corporate boardrooms. Few companies, however, have embedded NPS into an organization's ways of working as far as DFS has achieved. Stephenson admits that the metric isn't perfect, but he believes that its simplicity and the ability of everyone across the business to focus around a single metric significantly outweigh any downsides. As a result, NPS has become as important as the sales and profit figures throughout DFS, from front-line sales teams, to head office support teams, to senior executives and non-executive directors. By 2014, DFS's uses of NPS looked something like this:

- The company now collects over 200,000 separate customer reviews each year, covering various stages of its customer experience—pre-sales, point of sale, point of delivery, six months post-delivery, and following a customer service issue. This represents a response rate of over 10 percent.
- Each sales consultant, store team and manager, area, region, delivery team and individual members, the in-house factory teams and the online team, and call center service team receive weekly NPS reviews, and their performance bonuses are directly based on their average NPS scores.
- The executive team reviews overall NPS performance each week alongside sales, with actions identified for immediate resolution. Similarly, the monthly board meeting contains a review of the company's NPS performance.
- Any individual customer score of 6 or below results in a notification to the relevant store manager, who is expected to immediately follow up with the customer and then report to senior management on how the issue has been dealt with.
- Stephenson ensures that customers' answers are as honest as possible. Here are three steps they've taken to ensure the integrity of the data:
  - DFS provides a charitable donation for every response received. Stephenson found that the previous method of encouraging responses, which was to enter respondents

into a prize draw, had slightly skewed responses upward, whereas a charitable donation had no such impact.

o The entire system is administered by an independent third-party marketing agency, which is highlighted on all e-mails. Again, this has been found to improve the quality and integrity of customer responses.

o The system is e-mail based, but for those customers where no e-mail is collected, the marketing agency takes their mobile phone numbers to gain a sample of results from these customers to ensure that their views are in line with the majority of e-mail customers and also ensures that individual sales consultants are not "gaming" the system.

In other words, the NPS system that DFS has developed has become the oxygen that is breathed across the business. Rather than pursuing the development of large but intermittent initiatives that tend to follow annual customer surveys, the DFS system allows managers and colleagues from across the organization to make thousands of individual decisions every day that, together, have transformed the company and enabled it to be truly customer-centered.

That's not to say that there haven't been any bigger projects. Early on, for example, the poor NPS scores associated with the delivery teams led to a complete restructuring of the delivery service, with a far greater focus on evening and weekend deliveries. Elsewhere, a low NPS score was identified against a certain product. There had been very few complaints made against these sofas from customers, but it was clear that buyers were far from happy. As managers probed further, it became clear that the cushions were losing their comfort after a few months. Changes to the cushions on the sofa transformed the NPS scores, and sales of the product.

But it is the everyday decisions and actions that, according to Stephenson, have made the biggest difference. Everyone across the retail chain is now focused on working out how they can provide a better experience for their customers and earn their loyalty. Unsurprisingly, in the space of two years, DFS's overall NPS score went from that of a laggard to that of a class leader, with certain individual stores and consultants consistently delivering truly outstanding results. What's more, Stephenson and his team have been able to directly track sales improvements against the rise in NPS, delivering a return on investment from the system that has the enthusiastic support of all the shareholders. When Filby and Stephenson first proposed the NPS system, there were many skeptics across the DFS management team; a few years later, no one wanted to do without this critical resource.

It took Stephenson and his team three years to develop an integrated NPS system that established and embedded customer focus at DFS. Here are seven steps you can take to gain rapid, reliable, and relevant customer feedback from your customers and hardwire your people and your organization into your customers' everyday needs:

1. **Keep it Simple.** A simple measure, such as NPS, is easy for everyone across a business to understand and get behind. It is also easier to gain feedback from customers. DFS start with the NPS question but also ask up to 25 further questions in their survey. Even so, Stephenson suggests that the key to maximizing return rates is to ensure that the survey takes less than 5 minutes to complete;

2. **Start Small, Learn Fast.** It can be tempting to launch an organization-wide system immediately. You would be far better off, however, starting with a specific area of your business. This might be a particular customer group, product area, distribution channel, or geographical area. Starting small enables you to try new things, make quick adjustments, and work out what approach is likely to work best both for your customers and your organization as a whole.

3. **Work with a Partner.** Using an external partner to collect and analyze the results has two benefits. First, it enables you to learn from experts who have significant experience in this kind of work. Second, it allows you to send a message to your customers that their responses will be completely confidential and independently scrutinized.

4. **Focus on Frequency.** Hardwiring into your customers' needs is not an annual event; it needs to be a constant and instantaneous flow of information and decision making. The greater the frequency with which you are checking your customers' pulse, the smaller the adjustments you need to make and the faster you will reach your goal.

5. **Use the Same Metrics Across Your Company.** Whether you use NPS or a different system, you should use the same metrics across the business. That way everyone is focused on the same goal. It's no use keeping your customer satisfaction and feedback results on the executive corridor; you will only gain the results you want when everyone has ownership for improving your customers' experience.

6. **Integrate with Your Reward System.** At DFS, apart from a few central administrative staff, everyone's bonus is directly related to their own NPS score. Even sales consultants can only obtain their sales bonus if they reach a certain level of NPS performance.

7. **Ensure Independence and Integrity.** While most people in DFS are targeted on improving the NPS score and improving the experience of the company's customers, Stephenson is only targeted on delivering a robust and reliable system. As HR Director, he has no potential conflict of interest and can, instead, guarantee that the results are completely reliable and valid. This approach creates organizational trust in the scores, ensuring that managers across DFS are focused on improving shopper satisfaction and not trying to game the system or challenge others' results.

The key to success at DFS has been the company's ability to integrate customer feedback into the day-to-day management and operation of the business. Store colleagues, store managers, delivery teams, and more senior managers have a "real time" understanding of how well they are satisfying customers and can take corrective action as they proceed. The time lag between customer feedback and the company's response to that information continues to reduce and this rapid cycle of improvement is at the heart of what helps an organization to continue to be both first and fast.

CHAPTER 8

Sustaining Success and Kicking On

How Fast Is Too Fast?

This book is focused on helping you create a faster, more agile organization that is better able to cope with fast-changing and turbulent modern markets. There is a point, however, where your attempts to increase speed can actually have a negative effect on performance. Like a sprinter who tries to run too quickly in a race, starts to lose balance and who may even fall to the ground, organizations can also overstretch themselves in their bid for rapid growth and success.

The key is to find a pace that delivers sustainable success and improvement and that, over time, you can continue to increase without risking the collapse of your organization's ability to function. Don't get me wrong: the dangers of insufficient speed far outweigh the risks of excessive speed—and many more athletes lose races by being unable to run quickly enough than by running too fast—but each business has its own optimal speed based on its unique situation, capabilities, and culture.

In the previous seven chapters, I have given you the tools and frameworks to build and develop the maximum speed for your company, but what are the indicators that you may be trying to go too fast for your own good? Here are six factors that you should look out for

1. **No "No!"** I have continually argued in this book that you cannot sustainably move at pace if you don't focus. Or, as Richard Baker, the former CEO of Boots the Chemists, put it in Chapter 2, "You can't spray and sprint." One of the biggest ways that organizations stumble when they're trying to sprint is by trying to do too much

at once. If the answer to any new idea is always "Yes!" then you will find that nothing of any consequence is really delivered quickly. I have lost count of the number of times I have seen companies fail to deliver their key priorities simply because they have taken on too much, too soon. A lot of energy is used in trying to drive the initiatives forward, but much of this energy ends up as heat, in the form of frustration, rather than higher levels of performance. *How many strategic and other cross-functional projects is your organization currently pursuing, and what proportion of new idea proposals are approved for implementation?*

2. **Consistently Missed Milestones.** It may seem counterintuitive to accept that missing milestones is an indicator of trying to drive your organization too hard and too fast. I fully accept that failing to achieve your delivery timetable can simply be a function of poor project management. Yet, if you look at your milestone success rate in the context of the other six factors listed here, you may start to understand that the real problem is that you're asking your organization to take on more than it can actually handle. At one telecoms business I worked with, for instance, a major reorganization of the company's retail business consistently missed its early implementation milestones. As the retail leadership team reviewed the situation, it quickly became clear to them that both the retail operations team, and the human resources department, were so busy trying to implement other projects, they had not really bought into this new reorganization and were not focused on its delivery. Consequently, the retail director postponed the implementation of new IT systems and delayed the launch of a new service offering by two months so that the retail team could focus on delivering the fundamental reorganization of the management structures. *What is the success rate of the key milestones of your major strategic projects, and do your people genuinely have the capacity to focus on their delivery?*

3. **No One Knows the Priorities Anymore.** Companies that want to move and act quickly can be chaotic. Long hours and long agendas are common and the environment is demanding on everyone. If you try to move too quickly, people can become overwhelmed and not really know or understand your organization's real priorities. Add to

this the fact that managers generally find resolving urgent issues a far more attractive use of their working day than tackling longer term, proactive strategic projects, and you have the potential for an organization to start to collectively forget what's really important anymore. I've even had chief executive officers who cannot remember their company's top strategic projects simply because they have become so immersed in all the urgent stuff that can consume companies that seek to become faster-paced. If the CEO has this problem, the rest of his or her colleagues have no chance of knowing or pursuing the company's priorities: the organization has become, in effect, a collection of busy fools. *How well and how often do you communicate your organization's top priorities, and how well do your managers and colleagues focus on delivering them?*

4. **Endemic Errors.** As with point 2, consistently missed milestones, poor quality performance, and a high rate of errors could simply be a symptom of poor management. That said, if you find some consistent trends in poor quality performance alongside some of the other items in this list, endemic errors can also be a sign of a company that is trying to move too quickly. Some of these errors may be easy to put right. For example, I remember once seeing a sign in a recently opened Prêt-A-Manger restaurant in Nottingham that apologized to customers for its closure, with an explanation that the company had simply made a mistake and opened up too many outlets in the city and so had to close a couple of them to better reflect demand. In other circumstances, the number and scale of errors can be more serious. As we saw in Chapter 6, for instance, Tesco's rapid rollout of its Fresh & Easy concept failed to take into account some significant flaws in the format's customer offer and business model, costing the retailer nearly $2 billion in operating losses and write-offs. *To what extent are your major initiatives consistently incurring errors, and what review points do you have in place to ensure that they are in line with your customers' priorities and make commercial sense?*

5. **No Thinking Beyond the Current Quarter.** In many fast-paced businesses, the pressure to deliver "now" can be almost unbearable. Like a fire crew rushing to put out a blaze before immediately going onto the next emergency, the short-term focus can become

institutionalized. Little, if any effort is focused on thinking ahead about what's needed next. The acid test for me is to ask a company's most senior managers who in the organization is responsible for delivering ideas that will drive the growth of the business beyond the next 12 to 18 months. If the answer to that question is a blank stare, I know that the company's focus on short-term pace is damaging its chances of longer-term success. *So, who in your organization is directly responsible for driving growth beyond the next 12 to 18 months?*

6. **Stress Becomes Distress.** In this book I have consistently praised Amazon as a company where there is focus, pace, and agility. In many ways, Amazon is an exemplar of the modern fast-paced business and offers many lessons for the leaders of other organizations. In the summer of 2015, however, the New York Times ran an article highlighting the downsides of working at Amazon. In particular, the article, and subsequent discussions, highlighted the impact of the stress caused by the company's high expectations on Amazon's people. As Bo Olson, one former employee put it, "Nearly every person I worked with, I saw cry at their desk." If Mr. Olson's and similar claims are true, then Amazon's leadership team has a major legal and ethical issue to manage. But the issue is also economic. Research has shown that high stress levels mean that people do not operate effectively or efficiently: everything simply becomes "too much." As a leader of your business, it is essential that you remove drivers of "distress" and enable your teams to work at their most productive levels of stress. Over time, of course, you can also work with your people to help build their personal and technical capabilities so that they can reasonably and sustainably handle higher levels of stress, and further improve their pace and productivity. *What are your formal and anecdotal indicators saying about the level of stress across your business, and what actions are you taking to find the most productive stress levels?*

Moving Onto New Heights

The danger for most companies, of course, is not that they are moving too quickly, but that they are too slow. We started the book with a description of the decline and fall of Nokia and it is often the most successful organizations where calcification can be most pronounced. Nokia's decline was not inevitable. Other corporations have been able to sustain a leadership position more successfully than Nokia—or Kodak, HMV, RIM, and Olivetti for that matter—in the face of rapidly evolving markets. Companies such as Nike, BMW, Microsoft, P&G, and Goldman Sachs have consistently led their chosen markets over a sustained period.

But what are the specific differences in the underlying beliefs and values that prevent some companies from continuing to prosper, while others manage to sustain and improve their performance and pace? Critically, it's not a question of knowledge or insight—Kodak was one of the first companies to develop digital photography technology, and Nokia's scientists developed technologies that were the equal of other players. Instead, the solution is all about attitude.

I was once leading a major change program and, as part of the work, our team visited Crotonville, GE's leadership development campus just north of New York City. One of the center's directors had a photo of a lion attacking a gazelle in his office. Underneath the photo, it said, "It doesn't matter if you are the lion or the gazelle. When the sun comes up you'd better be running!" In other words, whether you're the leader of your market or a competitor from the pack of followers, you have to be willing to move as quickly as possible every single day if you are to continue to survive and prosper. This attitude forms part of what I call the "challenger mind-set," which is just as critical to the ongoing success of an existing market leader, like Nokia, as it is to a start-up business such as Innocent Drinks.

Moving onto new heights is the antithesis of staying in the cultural danger zone that we discussed in Chapter 2. In my experience, the vast majority of leaders want to make their mark on the world and leave a legacy of success. Problems arise when one of two situations occur. First, as we have discussed, leaders can be so fearful of failure that they aren't prepared to take the prudent risks that are necessary to succeed. In soccer parlance, they try and play for a draw rather than the win. The second problem arises when the leader becomes so enamored with their organization's success that he or she genuinely starts to believe that it is untouchable. Arrogance and hubris sets in and the organization starts to lose touch with its customers, its markets, and, in some cases, reality.

Bad news is not often tolerated in these businesses and the messenger, rather than the message, can become the target.

Both of these situations—a fear of failure and the establishment of hubris—create organizational inertia. Moving onto new heights and sustaining success demands that you prevent this inertia from building and demolishing it where it already exists. Here are seven steps you need to take to make this happen:

1. **Mix Confidence with Humility.** As we have seen, arrogance acts as a lead weight to your organization's growth rocket. Consistently successful businesses and business leaders find a way to mix an inner confidence and determination with a level of humility about the company's success to date. There is a collective belief that growth will happen, but nothing is taken for granted. Your organization's attitude on this issue starts at the top. As one of my CEO clients once said to me, "If I am not questioning and challenging our performance and our future plans, who will?" A little bit of paranoia can be a good thing, but only if it is joined at the hip with an equally optimistic view that anything is possible and that you genuinely believe that your people will find a way to succeed at pace.

2. **Have Goals that are Constantly Out of Reach.** One way of maintaining your humility is to have a goal that is constantly just out of reach. When I was a child and using the monkey bars on the climbing frame, I had to leave go with one hand in order to reach out to the next bar. It is the same with business, but only if you have a bar you wish to reach out for. A stretching, overarching goal acts as this bar, freeing you from your current position and enabling you to reach out beyond your current comfort zone. This means that you should be setting your next big goal before you have achieved your current goal. You do not want to be stuck hanging in the middle of the monkey bars, waiting to work out where you're going next. That only leads to a loss of momentum, making it far more difficult to reach the next bar.

3. **Constantly Ask "What If?"** The most valuable thing about continuously having stretching and challenging goals is that it forces you to think about doing things differently. If you set your goals

effectively, you won't be able to achieve them simply by doing better what you're already doing. A compelling goal demands that you question everything, and the best question to ask yourself is, "What if?" This question is optimistic, open, and leads to new possibilities. *What if* we developed that new service? *What if* we entered that new market? *What if* we formed an alliance with that business? Each of these questions encourages imagination, propelling you to create a future world. Your answer is not going to be "Yes" or "No," but will be an exploration of future ideas that could accelerate the success of your business.

4. **Focus on Innovation, Not Perfection.** Customers have never been so demanding, and your operational delivery standards must continue to be extremely high if you are to retain existing customers and attract new business. And yet, if you become completely fixated on perfecting your existing operating model, you will fail to rise to the challenge of fast-changing technologies, customer needs, and market competitors. I feel sure that Kodak's R&D team was still perfecting the company's patented film technology as it filed for bankruptcy amid the unstoppable rise of digital photography. Your market situation may not be as fast moving as that faced by Kodak's management and there is, of course, a need for you to balance your organization's efforts between current operational performance and future innovation. But, if you are a leader of your business and you want to accelerate your company's growth and profitability, you cannot allow your diary or your "mind space" to become dominated by how you simply fix and sort out current problems; you must find a way to spend significant time and effort on creating future growth ideas and developments.

5. **Work Customer-Back, Not Financials-Forward.** Companies that succeed over a long period have a strong financial base. They don't take stupid risks and they look to manage potential downsides to their activities. Strong financial management can, however, lead to a stranglehold on innovation. I have simply been in too many meetings in large corporate businesses where the financial team question every specific action and, in the absence of receiving cast-iron guarantees about a new initiative's likely future performance, downgrade

their forecast of the idea's impact and, as a result, reduce the level of investment and attention it will receive. This approach only reduces the chances of your organization's future viability. Instead, you should always—and I mean always—start with what will have the biggest positive impact on your customers and work backward. The business model can wait and can be worked on, but only if you have an idea that actually adds to your customers' lives.

6. **Pay Attention to the Weak Signals.** Similarly, successful businesses have teams of people who are entirely focused on producing and analyzing management reports. These reports cover sales, margins, cost performance, returns on investment, customer satisfaction, market share and operational efficiency, speed, waste, and effectiveness. Most managers are focused on the big, important numbers; the averages. For example, they will ask whether overall market share is moving up or down and respond accordingly. Unfortunately, markets aren't disrupted—at least initially—through the averages. Instead, they are disrupted at the margins. It is your innovative and early adopter customers who are likely to respond first to any new competitor or offering in your market. These customers may not form a significant part of your sales, but they could hugely influence your future prospects. You need to find a way to tune into these customer, market, and competitor changes at the fringes of your operations. Like an astronomer searching the night skies for new stars and galaxies, you need to look out for and pay attention to the weak signals.

7. **Ruthlessly Remove the Weeds.** Even with a relentless ambition and great new ideas, your ability to move with speed and precision will only happen if you have an organization that can deliver. In most successful companies, the creation of new functions and, in particular, bigger head office departments can serve to slow down innovation and action. There are simply too many people involved in decisions that you cannot make the rapid progress you're after. A great leader needs to vigorously remove the organizational "weeds." This means keeping organizational structures and processes as simple as possible, removing poor-performing managers and those that are actively preventing the corporate goals from being delivered, rationalizing the range of products and services you offer so that you are

not supporting activities that simply do not pay their way, and rapidly halting or amending initiatives that are failing to deliver.

The task of removing organizational inertia is, as you may have gathered, relentless. Like Sisyphus, the king from Greek mythology who was condemned for eternity to roll a huge rock up a hill, only to watch it roll back down again, you will need to attack inertia, today, tomorrow, and for every day you are a leader of your business. The work will never end, but the results can create a legacy of success and growth. What's more, your ability to step change the speed and pace of your business need not take an eternity to achieve; you can make big strides immediately.

Seven Immediate Steps You Can Take Today

So where do you start to help your company become "first" and "fast," both the leader of your market and its most dynamic innovator? And how can these actions become a symbol of the new organization you're seeking to develop? Each of the following seven actions will not only improve the speed and responsiveness of your company, but they can also be delivered rapidly. You can make them happen today and reinforce the message to your team, your organization, and maybe even to yourself, that rapid results are possible and that you don't need to wait 12 months before you see tangible improvements.

1. **Develop, Share, and Commit to New Behavioral Expectations.** In Chapter 2, I shared Richard Baker's memo to his team that he produced on his first day as chief executive of Boots the Chemists. What would your equivalent memo look like? What are your key areas of focus for the behaviors you want to see that will step change the pace and energy of your team and organization? Take the time to identify the top five behavioral changes you're after and be as specific as possible in your note. Baker, for example, included the following points that supported his commitment to organizational speed: *No one in the company works faster than we do; We start and finish meetings on time and we set a stretching example to others at all times; We must demand the impossible, set stretch goals and be unreasonable to get the job*

done; We will encourage brevity and simplicity. Complexity is the enemy of pace. Less is more; and Encourage people to have fun. Critically, once you have shared your expectations, personally commit to them. Be unstinting and disciplined in your adherence to the behaviors you're after so that you become a symbol of the new team or organization you're seeking to lead.

2. **Clarify Your #1 Goal.** In Chapter 4, we laid out the "strategy arrow." In this model the arrowhead, the cutting edge of your strategy, is your #1 goal. As we have seen, clarifying and committing to an overarching performance goal can transform the speed and effectiveness at which you can deliver your strategy. Your goal should be directly related to your financial performance, but it need not be financial. In fact, it tends to have more emotional resonance across organizations where it is nonfinancial. Here are five steps you can take to identify your #1 goal:

   • Bring your top team together and brainstorm a list of possible #1 goals for your team or business.

   • Review the pros and cons of each option and create a short list of two or three high-potential goals and, for each, establish a potential level of stretch ambition for the next 3 to 5 years.

   • Share these potential goals with selected managers and stakeholders from across your business. Ask for their feedback to understand which goals engage your people and which leave them cold, and to understand the balance between a stretch ambition and the level at which your people no longer believe the goal is credible.

   • Review the feedback with your top team and select your #1 goal and its associated level of ambition.

   • Use the #1 goal to (1) Establish annual and quarterly goals that will enable you to track the progress of your success; (2) Review your strategic agenda and to determine which of your key initiatives best support its delivery, with a view to accelerating these projects; (3) Share the goal with your subteams and ask them to create their own #1 goal that will best support its delivery.

3. **Create Unambiguous Accountabilities and Objectives.** A key theme of Chapter 3 was the critical importance of clear, instantaneous,

and unambiguous accountabilities. You must therefore critically review your existing accountabilities, identify and tackle areas where there are overlaps, committee-based accountabilities, and uncertainties. You should, of course, start with your own team. In many instances, clarifying accountabilities will lead to a reduction in the number of leaders. You may lose some good people as part of this process, but in my experience, a smaller, focused, and more accountable team can achieve a lot more, far more quickly, than a bigger, less clearly accountable group or committee.

4. **Review and Reduce Your List of Major Projects.** My own rule of thumb is that most organizations, at any one time, are running twice as many major projects as they can reasonably deliver at pace. This heuristic is relevant in even the biggest organizations, and in Chapter 6, I set out the need to focus your resources and efforts where you can have the biggest impact. Having established your #1 goal and clarified your senior accountabilities, you are in a far better position to review your list of projects and initiatives and determine which you should really get your collective shoulders behind. In descending order, here are the five criteria that I would use to rank your strategic projects:

   • *Impact on your #1 goal.* What difference will this project make to the delivery of your most important goal?

   • *Ability to make material progress in the next 3 to 6 months.* What level of improvement is possible in the next few months with dedicated focus and resource driving this initiative?

   • *Customer impact.* How will the project directly improve the experience you deliver for your customers?

   • *Internal organizational fit.* How well does this initiative fit with the capabilities and culture of the organization, and how engaged will your people be in delivering its benefits?

   • *Risk.* What is the worst-case scenario of this project and its related investment?

5. **Identify and Pursue Your Top Priority For the Next 90 Days.** In Chapter 6, I described how Boots the Chemists had created momentum and growth on the back of a three-month focus on improving stock availability. This initiative allowed the company to deliver

rapid, material, and sustainable profit improvement in just 90 days, and formed the basis for further growth. On the back of your review set out in point 4, above, I recommend that you choose the project that best combines an ability to deliver a significant impact on your #1 goal and that enables you to make a real noticeable difference in performance in the next three months. You can then communicate its importance to your teams, and organize for the delivery of the benefits, using the project as a demonstration of what a step change in the pace of your business could actually mean for your business.

6. **Increase the Frequency and Discipline of Your Progress Reviews.** I mentioned in Chapter 6 how the leadership team of U.K. grocer, Asda, undertook Monday morning meetings to review progress of their latest growth projects as a key part of their revival in the early 1990s. Similarly, Amazon ran weekly sessions to review and assess their latest, big ideas. Monthly or quarterly reviews of key projects suggest that pace is not such a big issue for your business. Weekly sessions at the highest possible level to review progress of your most important priorities will raise the energy, pace, and momentum of these initiatives, helping them to deliver benefits far faster than perhaps they currently achieve. These sessions need not last hours, or require the usual reports and documentation. Instead, they can and should have simple administration so that your focus is on ensuring that they make a material impact as quickly as possible.

7. **Introduce a New, Faster Innovation Process.** In Chapter 5, I shared some faster approaches to managing innovation. I believe that you can send a clear signal to your people, as well as accelerate the delivery of new, profitable revenue growth by developing an approach to innovation that is slicker, quicker, and more action-focused. There are three critical success factors. First, ensure that someone who has the freedom to say "Yes" or "No" to the development of specific proposals leads the process. This person may be the chief executive or your top sales or marketing executive, but a clear decision-maker and leader of the business must lead the process. Second, the process should be as transparent as possible, and open to any ideas from anywhere inside the company. New ideas aren't just the gift of a few product development specialists, and opening up the process

to everyone increases your chance of finding a dynamic new idea. Third, firmly place the focus on rapid action. Having a small fund to support the development of simple, early prototypes, for example, stops the process from being conceptual and accelerates your ability to learn directly from customers.

These seven actions alone have the potential to transform the speed at which your organization responds to the speed of change in your markets. They are unlikely to be the end of the change required to move and act faster, but they are a great place to start. Throughout this book I have sought to give you pragmatic ways to move and act faster, helping your business to achieve and sustain market leadership positions during turbulent times and these seven actions demonstrate that you can start that journey now, regardless of the challenges you face. What's more, engaging in the development of a faster, more responsive, and more agile organization is not only necessary, it is also meaningful. It is a task that will provide your organization with the capability to survive and succeed in a fast-changing, uncertain world. Its survival and success will only happen, however, if you start now. There's no time to waste. What are you waiting for?

Index

CPSIA information can be obtained
at www.ICGtesting.com
Printed in the USA
FSOW03n0446280416
19769FS